HIDDEN WINGS

HIDDEN WINGS

EMERGING FROM TROUBLED TIMES WITH NEW HOPE AND DEEPER WISDOM

MARGARET SILF

Augsburg Books

MINNEAPOLIS

For Kirstin, with my love always,
from forest floor to forever flight

First published in Great Britain in 2017 by
Darton, Longman and Todd Ltd

© 2017 Margaret Silf

The right of Margaret Silf to be identified as the Author of this work has been
asserted in accordance with the Copyright, Designs and Patents Act 1988.

HIDDEN WINGS
Emerging from Troubled Times with New Hope and Deeper Wisdom

Cover image: © iStock 2020: Collection of Hand Drawn black silhouette
butterflies by Valeriya Pichugina
Cover design: Emily Drake

Print ISBN: 978-1-5064-6201-1
eBook ISBN: 978-1-5064-6729-0

CONTENTS

Acknowledgements 7

PRELUDE: THE START OF THE STORY 9
An innocent question 11

PART 1: CATERPILLAR KINGDOM 23
An egg is laid ... 25
Family life 29
The world is our takeaway 32
Corridors of power 36
All in this together 45
Afterthoughts 49

PART 2: DISINTEGRATION 51
A disenchanted forest 53
Growing out of ourselves 56
Winding down, or waking up? 60
Fed up. Hung up. 62
The Elephant Room 66
The Story Circle 69
Afterthoughts 76

PART 3: THE EDGE OF THE CLIFF 79
Lights out 81
Drawing the curtains 84
Dancing in the dark 87

Embroiled in the chaos   90
Strangely attracted   95
Cousin Moth   98
Afterthoughts   103

PART 4: IMAGINAL DREAMING   105
To sleep, perchance to dream   107
The space for hope   111
The power of one   115
Chains of kindness   119
Walls and bridges   122
The bigger picture   126
Afterthoughts   129

PART 5: EMERGENCE   131
Birth struggle   133
Taking flight   137
Giving and taking   141
The travel bug   145
Imagining the future   148

POSTLUDE: TAKING IT FURTHER   153

ACKNOWLEDGEMENTS

A sincere word of thanks

To David Moloney, Helen Porter and Judy Linard at Darton, Longman and Todd, for all your warm encouragement, wise guidance, careful editing and creative design that has gone into the production of this book.

To Louis M. Savary, for your invaluable insights into, and interpretation of, the thought of Teilhard de Chardin and for your personal encouragement when we met.

To Marianne and Robin Anker-Petersen, for making me so welcome at your home in Perth, Scotland over the years, and for giving me much-appreciated writing space at The Bield in which the proposal for this book took shape

To Benedicte Scholefeld and Kath Saltwell for helping me to focus on the theme, and to all who participated in the early 'Butterfly' retreats at the Ammerdown Centre, Somerset, and Emmaus House, Edinburgh.

To Jane Besly and Annette White, for being such enthusiastic and inspirational early readers of the draft.

To Mary Saucier and my friends at the FCJ Centre in Calgary and all who took up the challenge there to 'grow into tomorrow', and to Trish and Richard Young in Edmonton for your hospitality, solidarity and friendship, especially through the night of June 23rd 2016 and its aftermath.

And, very specially, to Kirstin and Paul, Alexa and Isabella, for keeping me on track during times when the world seems dark, and for helping me to stay mindful of what matters most.

PRELUDE
THE START
OF THE STORY

'I dwell in possibility'

Emily Dickinson

AN INNOCENT QUESTION

'Grandma, do you know what *mettyfourmiss* means?'

The question insists on clambering aboard my train of thought that was sleepily chugging its way through a leisurely breakfast, as I attempt to decipher what she is trying to say, with her six-year-old linguistic limitations and her Ayrshire accent.

'I think you might have to run that by me again', I urge her gently.

By the severalth time of unpacking I get a glimpse of it…

'Are you trying to say "metamorphosis"?' I suggest.

Her eyes light up. Finally. Grandma gets it. 'Met a more fose is', she repeats, slowly and deliberately. And then with obvious disbelief, 'Do *you* know what a "metamorefose" is?'

'It's about transformation,' I respond, trying, without great success, to suppress any suggestion of superior knowledge. 'Have you been doing caterpillars and butterflies at school?' I ask. 'Because that's a story about metamorphosis, about change and transformation. In fact it's *the best story*.'

She beams her infant approval all over me, unable quite to digest the enormity of the fact that her latest discovery might also have penetrated the dense defences of the grandmaternal mind.

'My teacher doesn't know how to spell "met a more fose is"', she announces. 'She told us so.'

Silencing my inner protest that this person who can't spell

metamorphosis should have been trusted with the education of my grandchild, I leap instinctively to the teacher's defence:

'Oh, I think she was probably kidding you.'

'No', comes the instant reply. 'She wasn't kidding. She had to look it up on her iPad.'

Against such damning evidence what more can be said? Game, set and match to the iPad. Over and Out. And with that she turns her attention to weightier matters, and 'metamorphosis' is left hanging, waiting quietly for its time to come.

There will be quite a bit of hanging about in our story.

What is the 'more' in metamorphosis?

She had one thing right. There is *more* to this mystery than we could ever guess. In fact there is a quantum leap right at the heart of it, as one creature changes physically into quite another. What begins as one that crawls becomes one who flies. What begins as an all-consuming grub, destroying the very plant that feeds it, becomes one who touches creation lightly and pollinates the plants on which it alights. The potential death-dealer becomes the life-giver. Some people call that 180 transformation. Religious traditions might call it *metanoia*, or conversion from a lower to a higher state of being. Spiritual explorers call it the emergence of higher levels of consciousness in the human family through the process of *spiritual evolution*.

What changes this from mere intellectual speculation into a roadmap for the future of all creation on this planet is that this *more* is revealing itself precisely in the times when it feels as though everything is falling apart and collapsing in on itself. We are living through such times right now and we have never been more urgently in need of a spiritual roadmap.

The 'more' in metamorphosis is nothing less than the human potential for spiritual, as well as physical, evolution. And the

SPIRITUAL EVOLUTION

Many spiritual explorers, notably the late French Jesuit paleontologist Pierre Teilhard de Chardin, have suggested that humanity is engaged in a journey not simply of physical, but also spiritual evolution. This proposes that we are, step by step, moment by moment moving closer towards the best we can be, or further away from it, depending on the choices we make both individually and collectively.

Teilhard suggests that this evolutionary direction is governed by the law of attraction-connection-complexity-consciousness. Attraction leads to connection, in primitive life forms just as in human persons. When simpler life forms combine they create a heightened complexity. The final stage of this process in human life is the raising of consciousness. Human beings are manifestations of the universe becoming conscious of itself. Nothing is static. It is either e-volving or de-volving – emerging or regressing.

The caterpillar story is a living example of this process in action, as a self-focused consuming insect transforms, through chaotic breakdown, into a life-giving 'flying flower'.

secret is already latent deep inside us. It may, however, be willing to reveal itself if we coax it into a conversation. So this is where our story begins. And to get the true inside story, we will invite an *imaginal cell* to be our narrator.

An extraordinary guide

What, you may well be asking, is an imaginal cell?

Before we embark on our journey of discovery, it's important to appreciate a bit of biology that stunned me with its significance when, not so long ago, I was introduced to it by a friend in Australia. Some readers will be well aware of the role of the imaginal cell in the caterpillar story. To others it may come as a complete surprise, as it did to me. The biology is relatively simple to grasp. The wider significance of such a phenomenon may direct us to a much bigger story than the drama being played out in our gardens every summer.

Here's the biology story ...

Some cells within the caterpillar, although sharing the same DNA, differ from the majority of the cells in significant ways. Biologists report that they 'resonate on a different frequency' from the others, and that they hold the blueprint for what will become the various parts of the future butterfly. These are the *imaginal cells*. They are called 'imaginal' not because they are in any way 'imaginary' (they are very real indeed), but because they hold the blueprint of the *imago*, the Latin term for the mature insect – for that very particular mature insect that will emerge from that particular caterpillar. They are also known as *imaginal discs*, because of their flat structure.

Initially the imaginal cells operate independently as single-cell organisms, but the caterpillar's immune system regards them as a threat and attacks them, drenching them in juvenile hormone to suppress their activation during the caterpillar stage of the cycle. The imaginal cells persist, however, multiply and begin to connect with each other forming clusters, and start to resonate at the new frequency of the emerging butterfly, sharing information among themselves. In the chrysalis stage, they reach critical mass, and begin to function as a coherent multi-cell organism as, in the fullness of time, they become the butterfly.

This is the biology. The wider implications, however, are very far-reaching indeed, which is why an imaginal cell will be our narrator of this unfolding story. Our imaginal cell carries a deeper wisdom that we need if we are to embrace the invitation to transformation that our times are pressing upon us, and for which most spiritual traditions seek to prepare us.

This imaginal wisdom warns us that the path to transformation will not be an easy one. It will bring us up against serious opposition; just as the prophetic voices all down the ages have been vilified and suppressed. But it also assures us that the call to a transformed life will always prevail over all the odds that are stacked against it. Opposition can kill the dreamer, as history repeatedly reveals, but it can never kill the dream. How urgently we need this reassurance in our present deeply troubled times, but it needs to be an *authentic* reassurance and no mere morale-boosting rhetoric from either politicians or pulpits. The caterpillar story is as real as it gets, literally growing in our own back yard. What can we learn from it? How might it bring genuine encouragement into our global disillusionment?

The imaginal wisdom also knows that, although we are currently groping our way through threatening, adversarial and deeply divisive situations, the time will come when the forces of such extreme opposition (the ordinary caterpillar cells) will become the very means of nourishing and enabling the new possibility. So profound is the change into which we are being invited that what appear to be its enemies will in time become its enablers.

The imaginal cell knows that the promise of transformation is both true and possible, as it carries the still unborn future deep within it. It also knows that the emergence of the new beginning only happens through the catastrophic meltdown (in the chrysalis) of the old order. It knows that this new order also depends on a change of attitude away from 'I can do this on my own' in favour of 'To make this a reality we need to work together'. It trusts what it knows deep inside itself, all through that breakdown, even when everything seems to shout the opposite message. It trusts the hidden wings it already contains but that it cannot, as yet, even imagine. Doesn't that sound rather like 'faith'?

Finally, the imaginal cell knows, against all the evidence to the contrary, that there is *more* to the caterpillar than even the caterpillar can guess. It will come as no surprise, therefore, to learn that the term *imaginal cell* is also sometimes applied to visionary leaders who imagine a better future for life on our planet and strive, with others, to make this future a reality. You may well think there is a conspicuous absence of such leaders in our world today; in fact they could probably be counted on the fingers of one hand. But consider these possibilities:

What if each of us is potentially an imaginal cell, carrying the still hidden seed of the best possible version of who we can become?

What if each one of us carries within us a fragment of a bigger story – the best possible version of humanity we can become, on this beautiful fragile planet we call home?

What if the '*extra*-ordinary' is always present and striving to emerge from our own very ordinary lives?

What if, as the opening quotation suggests, we too 'dwell in possibility'? What might such possibility become? How might we birth it into being?

An invitation to evolve

If we didn't have caterpillars we would have to invent them, because they provide a perfect metaphor – more than that, a *model* – of our own spiritual journey from all we are now to all we can become. This humble creature transforms, through metamorphosis, from a potentially destructive, all-consuming pest, to a beautiful and life-giving butterfly, taking flight, spreading life to all the flowers it pollinates and joy to all who see it. The metamorphosis of the caterpillar sounds incredible, and yet we see the evidence of it all around us every summer.

AN INNOCENT QUESTION

It's rather harder to believe that we too are in process of transformation, but unlike the caterpillar we have choices. We can work *with* the dynamic of transformation, or against it. The way we make our choices will determine the future of human life on planet Earth.

The miracle of metamorphosis in one species is just one facet of a much bigger story. All creation is in process of transformation. We call that process *evolution*. I once saw a sign in the Evolution section of the Paris Science Museum that stopped me in my tracks. It read: 'The process of hominization is probably still ongoing, but the process of *humanisation* has barely begun, and is still very fragile.' 'Hominization' describes the course of physical evolution. Humanisation is something else. It is not unreasonable to call it spiritual evolution. This book is about that process of humanisation – the challenge to become more and more fully human, ultimately transcending everything we think we are.

The bad news is that such transformation, such evolution, happens mainly through periods of apparent total breakdown. This is the pattern that the natural sciences clearly reveal. It is also the dynamic of change and growth that runs through our ancient spiritual traditions. What we have known, and grown used to, is *no longer*. Where we are going is *not yet*. There is no way to make the journey from *no longer* to *not yet* without going through chaotic breakdown.

Never has this process been more clearly in evidence than right now in our own times, when even the most phlegmatic and conservative citizens are becoming increasingly and disturbingly aware that enormous changes are happening that will affect us all in ways we are quite unable to predict. The climate has become seriously unstable. The planet is threatened. Our economic systems are failing. Brutal conflicts are precipitating mass migrations. Our politics are turning the world upside down in ways that may terrify and dismay us.

Recent electoral decisions in the UK and the US in particular have sent shock waves through the ordinary citizens of those countries and the wider world. There may be many more aftershocks to follow, because these developments are symptoms of a widespread reaction against the way things are in our world today. Protest votes may well lead to results that were neither intended nor desired, but their consequences remain the same: they blow apart existing certainties and leave us gasping for the fresh air that we both desire and dread.

It is in this state of extreme and potentially very dangerous uncertainty that this book was conceived. My hope is that it may, with the help of the caterpillar, and particularly the imaginal cell who will be our guide, give us a reason to trust the way ahead, to risk, however grudgingly, the chaos that engulfs us, and to make choices that prepare us to make the quantum leap beyond the impasse to a new stage of human life on this planet that at present we cannot even imagine.

Our human egg has fallen off the wall, like Humpty Dumpty. Nothing is going to put it back together again. The world is changing beyond recognition.

This would be an ending – if the egg simply fell to disaster.

But if the egg broke because it was *hatching*, then it's a new beginning.

If these thoughts resonate with you, just observe the disorder and confusion through which you – and all of us – are trying so hard to wade. Feel the broken shells crunch beneath your fretful feet. Let the regrets, the reproaches, the remorse be there. There is good reason to feel angry when your applecart has been tumbled. There may be every reason to resist and oppose the waves of destruction that the storm has unleashed. But keep in mind that all this turbulence may be both the *aftermath* of your shattered certainties and at the same time the *afterbirth* of new life hatching. Let our imaginal cell be your midwife during this arduous labour through which our nations, our world and we ourselves are struggling. She alone knows the miracle that is still hidden deep within us, and the new life that is straining to emerge out of all the pain.

METAMORPHOSIS

A profound and often fairly sudden biological change of physical form from one stage in the development of an organism to the next stage in its life cycle. In the case of the caterpillar this process marks the development of the organism from caterpillar to pupa (chrysalis) and from pupa to adult butterfly.

More generally the term metamorphosis can be used to define any change into something radically new, or any remarkable transformation. The term *transformation* itself defines the act of changing form, shape or appearance.

The caterpillar-butterfly life cycle is probably nature's most compelling example of metamorphosis.

Our imaginal cell now takes up the story in her own words.

Let her tell you your own story.

Let her tell you our human story.

Let her engage you in conversation and invite you into your own transformation.

PART 1
CATERPILLAR KINGDOM

'Life is something endlessly in the process of becoming something else'

Richard Holloway

AN EGG IS LAID ...

I begin my life in an egg that is smaller than a pinhead, yet my ancestors have been on Earth for 130 million years. We evolved here at much the same time as the flowers – lovely birthing partners. We have seen so much of life unfold here, including yourselves, our human cousins, who emerged less than a quarter of one million years ago. We are your elders, small though we are, and for this reason I wonder whether you might permit me to pass on some of the wisdom and experience we have learned along our long journey through the aeons to today.

You too began your human journey as just a single fertilised cell. You too were just the size of a pinhead. But that cell, like mine, held all the potential of everything you would become. Just like the entire universe, our common home, which, it's thought, began as a tiny power-pack of compressed energy no bigger than a grain of salt, and yet containing, in potential, everything that would ever unfurl into the seemingly infinite space we now know we inhabit. Everything connects. From the crawling caterpillar to the expanding universe. Everything connects.

And this is how it is with us, the caterpillar cells, at the beginning of *our* story. All the potential, packed into that little egg, was our parent butterfly's legacy to us as she died. But at our beginning none of us knows the butterfly that laid us, or even the caterpillar we are destined to become. We are still contained in a small but well-defended little egg. We are laid with the utmost care by our parent in a safe place – usually the underside of a leaf, where predators will not easily find us and end our existence

EGG

Female butterflies lay many eggs, most of which will not survive. As they hatch, pupate and transform themselves, they already carry inside themselves, locked away in their imaginal cells, the butterfly they will become. The eggs are laid in a place safe from predators, usually on the underside of a leaf carefully chosen to provide exactly the right food for the hatching caterpillar. When it hatches, the larva gnaws open the egg shell with its jaws and eats the remainder of the egg as its first meal.

before it has really begun. More than that, as we will discover when we hatch, we have been laid on the perfect kind of leaf on which we most like to feed. That's what I call family planning.

But this is just biology, albeit biology that meshes with the whole story of the universe and reflects nature's way of getting things so right, if no one interferes with her. It still leaves a question hovering there above our heads (because it's not something we can 'get' with our minds) and quivering somewhere in our heart (which turns out to be the only way it makes sense). The question might be expressed like this: Is this whole enterprise energised by something we call 'love'? Or is it just the neutral, dispassionate unfolding of a biological process. The question leaves me, an imaginal cell, unimaginably miniscule, still curled up in the mother egg, pondering this huge mystery. Is it, or is it not, fundamentally about love?

As long as I merely reflect on the biology, the question just buzzes around in my mind, finding no answer more satisfying than the famous 'selfish gene' response. But the words 'neutral' and 'dispassionate' don't resonate on my frequency. (You will recall that we imaginal cells resonate on our own unique frequency, which is other than that of our fellow caterpillar cells.) It's when I listen to this frequency that I pick up on the jarring notes, and why they feel so dissonant. Something in the core of my cell remembers my origins, and that's what sets the quiver going in my heart.

There was a time before the egg. There was a parent butterfly who laid the egg. I can't imagine what a butterfly might be – not yet, not quite – but I feel her wings fluttering already in the still unformed creature I am becoming. As she flickers in and out of my emerging consciousness, I see passion. I see desire. I feel her longing for the flower that will give her the nectar that nourishes. And I feel the flower's longing for *her*, the creature who will pollinate it and make it fruitful into future generations, bringing joy to the earth. There is nothing neutral and dispassionate about this encounter. It is the result of attraction between two separate earthly creatures. It leads to an intimate connection between them and a symbiotic relationship in which both parties are enriched and neither is diminished.

And there is another kind of longing. As summer advances my father seeks out my mother, under the full power of sexual attraction. When they meet and recognise each other, they come together, they remain locked in the embrace of their coupling for up to an hour. Watch that encounter re-enacted in your own garden and you will see two beautiful, fragile creatures dancing in the air. In fact butterflies are sometimes called 'dancing flowers'. And how true that is. Nourished by the flowers, which they in turn bring to fruitfulness, they themselves dance together into the future. Once more there is attraction, leading to intimate connection. My egg is fertilised. The result will be another being. A being in a very different form, yet bringing forth a new beginning of the ancient story of itself, through the mystery of transformation. A more complex being who will make a unique journey to become the fullness of who it is. A being who will become another manifestation of the universe becoming conscious of itself.

Attraction leading to connection resulting in a creature of higher complexity and rising consciousness. Even in my embryonic state I sense that this process will be crucial to my own journey through life – and perhaps to yours too?

But for now, I rest in the egg, waiting for my time to come. There will be a lot of waiting in our story, but the result will be well worth the wait, so let us together seek the gift of patience and of trust. The one thing, above all, that I am learning to trust, here in my egg, is that this story is *a love story*, transcending, by far, its mere biological facts.

All creatures, especially human creatures have a heart that is able to quiver. What does *your* heart do when you ponder the mysteries of your beginning? Do they speak to you of love as well as genes? Do you trust what you hear when you tune into your own imaginal wavelength?

FAMILY LIFE

The sum of all the cells that will form a caterpillar makes for quite a large family, and as in all families, each cell has its own life to lead, its own unique purpose, to become some part of the caterpillar anatomy. So far so good. We all share the same DNA, after all. Shouldn't that ensure that we are reasonably compatible? And it's true that most of the cells soon establish their own ways of communicating with each other. The Caterpillar Web is rapidly developed to keep everyone informed. And one of the first bits of breaking news to hit the headlines is this:

'Someone's out of step! Are we hosting resident aliens in our midst?'

You'll realise from this that there are voices influencing our news media that are, shall we say, prone to sensationalism, indifferent to truth, and a bit inclined to point the finger at the 'other' when things are going wrong. It's something we are going to have to look into, by and by, when our caterpillar economy is a bit more established.

This is the beginning of what seems like the Great Divide – though it isn't actually a 'divide', as we will discover. Rumours spread quickly. Some cells are marching to a different drumbeat, the gossip goes. They share the same DNA as all the other cells, but, so the experts report, they *resonate on a different frequency*.

And this is where the first chapter of my story begins, because I am one of those 'resident aliens'. In HumanWorld I would probably be detained at the airport. I am an imaginal cell, living and growing inside the developing caterpillar. I am not alone. There are many of us and we keep multiplying as cells are supposed to do, but the rest of the caterpillar community doesn't like us. Non-conformists like us are rarely tolerated in any community. Neither we, nor they, yet understand what is causing the rift. It will transpire that we are different because we are carrying a future mystery within us, that no one – least of all ourselves – yet understands or can possibly imagine. Ironic, really, that imaginal cells should be the ones whose future no one can imagine.

It feels lonely, being an imaginal cell, so massively are we outnumbered. Sometimes I feel I'm the only one around, and I long for some like-minded company – for others who are also tuned in to the secret mystery inside us. And that's how we communicate. We don't have anything so organised as the Caterpillar Web. We don't broadcast news to each other. We *sing* it. Or, more accurately, we *vibrate* it, on our own frequency. I can't describe the joy it releases in me when I pick up the resonance with other imaginal cells, and I am reassured that I'm not away with the fairies, day-dreaming some future that will never happen.

Ancient wisdom tells us that 'the Kingdom is within you'. Surely this is what it means – a mysterious, as yet unrevealed possibility of being is embedded deep within our nature, in the very core of our being.

And it's not an elitist, divisive thing. As my story unfolds, you will see that *all* the cells in CaterpillarWorld are ultimately destined to bring this mysterious future into being, each in its own unique way. You could say it's a microcosm, in the caterpillar community, of what is also evolving in the human community. You might even call it the secret of eternal life, or, at least, the secret of transformation. But we still have a long way to go before our story is told and it isn't going to be plain sailing.

And for all this fine talk and these high aspirations, right now, things are changing, and it isn't looking very good …

Crawl with me, if you are so minded, as we explore this, our caterpillar kingdom. The journey we will make is a journey through a hall of mirrors. If you look closely, you may see your own story, your country's story, and the world's story reflected back in shafts of piercing light and pools of impenetrable darkness. All are needed, if the story is to be told. Both light and shadow are there, in the heart of the imaginal cell. Both chaos and creation. A dance in which both partners engage – the things we dread and the things we long for.

Our story began with a dance, as our parent butterflies danced in the air in order to make fruitful the egg from which we emerged. It continues to dance through the light and the darkness, the yin and the yang, harmony and conflict. Ancient wisdom has always understood this. It has also always warned against debilitating fear, which alone has the power to strangle human loving:

'Don't be afraid', it enjoins us. 'Fear not the ending that you dread, for if you are mired in fear you may miss the new beginning that you long for.'

Does anything in your own story seem to be 'out of step'? Take note of it. It may be the most important thing of all, and it may be inviting you to listen and respond to it. But don't dismiss the rest of the music. Nothing is unnecessary in nature's economy. Everything plays its part in the emerging story. Every cell counts. We are all in this together ...

THE WORLD IS OUR TAKEAWAY

The next stage of our journey begins with a bite and a nibble. When the time is right we bite a hole in our egg and then nibble at it until we can clamber out.

We start as we mean to go on. From now on the agenda is 'Nibble and Grow'. We are ready to establish a whole new world, and take over the forest. We are ready to Make CaterpillarWorld Great Again. And as with all such megalomania, we take no account of the needs of the rest of creation. It's all about *us*.

Remember that the cells that are in charge at this stage are not the imaginal cells. Their time has not yet come. The cells-in-charge of this caterpillar empire are much the same, in many ways, as those of the human family. You might recognise the profile in the mirror. The colonisation. The exploitation. The relentless expansion.

For now, it's on with the nibble. Our first meal is our own egg. From then on we will eat everything that comes our way, including the leaf we are sitting on.

Such is our consuming fervour that for our last meal we will consume our very selves.

But that particular meltdown still lies in the future. I'm crawling ahead of myself.

Perhaps, for now, a word about the way we organise our caterpillar kingdom. A united kingdom, you might think. On that score you might want to reserve judgement. Certainly we appear to be united. Every cell contributes to the whole living organism of the caterpillar, even though we, the imaginal cells,

LARVA
The juvenile form of a creature after hatching from its egg and before metamorphosis into an adult. The caterpillar is in the larva stage, during which it is a wingless and voracious feeder. It passes through several 'moults' or sheddings, as it literally grows out of its skin.

are still dormant, for reasons that will become clear as we crawl on. Any community of cells like ours needs some kind of vision to drive and inspire and energise it. The body alone doesn't go anywhere, but it *embodies* a spirit or energy of something greater than its physical self. Whether that 'something' is life-giving in the context of the bigger picture, or diminishing of, or harmful to that picture, depends on the choices we make.

A caterpillar's scope for making choices is limited. For you, the human family, things are very different. Every choice each one of you ever makes will either enhance and expand the bigger picture or diminish and damage it. Your call! Our call, in this stage of our story, is just to keep on consuming and growing. That sounds pretty self-centred, and indeed it is. It has little regard for the wider world. In fact it can be devastating for the wider world, which in practice might be the bushes in your own back garden. We are regarded as pests by many. They may revise their opinion when we emerge as butterflies, but that is a while away. For now we are just pests.

Sometimes I try to imagine how our planet and its residents would appear from outer space (I am, after all, an imaginal cell and that's what we do). You have had the experience in human living memory of seeing that delicate blue-green orb hanging in the blackness of space, as seen by astronauts, and it changed something in the human psyche for ever. If we could take that experience further and reflect on how a greater consciousness than our own might view the way things are done on planet Earth, what might we pick up?

From such a perspective, it might well appear that human beings regard our planet (yes, *we* are residents too!) as one vast open-all-hours takeaway. You certainly seem to take away more than you give, if you'll forgive my boldness in mentioning it. You certainly seem to be out of control in your growth and expansion tendencies. You are squeezing out so many of the rest of us. Some species have even been forced out of existence altogether, and others have no room to move. You have even endangered the very conditions of life on our planet, through your reckless use of natural resources. The polar icecaps are melting. The sea levels are rising. Soon Washington and Westminster will be lakes again, in which fact lies a certain irony.

PUPA

The life stage of the caterpillar between the larva and the adult stages. During this stage the caterpillar stops eating and is encased in a chrysalis as it undergoes metamorphosis. This stage can last from a few days to many months.

You know all this of course. You have heard it too often, and you are doing what you can to stem the tide of destruction, I know that. But what you may not know is that there is more to the caterpillar feeding frenzy than meets the eye. Actually it's how caterpillars have to be at this stage in their story. They have to build themselves up, flesh themselves out, you might say, to make the space in which the next stage can begin. They are evolving before your eyes, even as you try to purge them out of your shrubbery. Try to forgive them the excesses, as you allow the next chapter of the story to take shape.

Before transformation can happen there has to be a form to transform. This is what the caterpillar is – the not very appealing form preparing for a different future. I even have to admit that while they are still in the caterpillar stage they need to keep the imaginal cells quiet, to prevent them from moving the story on too fast. You'll see, as we crawl on, how important it is going to be for them to go through the expansion stage, in which they will grow out of themselves several times over. But then – the crash, when they finally realise that enough is enough, as we will discover.

The human family especially in the affluent parts of the world, is still thoroughly embroiled in the global takeaway mentality. How do you feel about this yourself? Is this all you are, or is there a new chapter to come in your story too? Do you think humanity is evolving? The alternative, I humbly, from my forest leaf, suggest, is stagnation, followed by extinction, with no butterfly emerging. That would be rather a tragedy, don't you think?

CORRIDORS OF POWER

From the perspective of human dramatics, the management of a caterpillar community may appear to be simplicity itself. Not so: where two or more are gathered, whether they are human beings or caterpillars, there will be politics. So as your narrator and tour guide, may I invite you to sit in – a fly on the wall if you like – on a few interesting conversations with some of the head honcho cells in the higher echelons of caterpillar government? We'll begin at the ...

Ministry of Defence

It may come as no surprise to learn that most of our budget goes on defence. It's no different in your human communities. Our overweening sense of entitlement doesn't mean that we sleep peacefully on our leaves. The forest is full of threats. From our first day out of the egg we need all the defences our homeland security enforcers can provide. So I want to raise a few questions with the defence segment.

Your segment seems to demand an inordinate share of our caterpillar resources. What do you spend it on?

Well, as you know, the threats come in many different guises, so we plan our defence along three main fronts: disguise and deception, deterrence, and pre-emptive strikes. We disguise ourselves by concealing ourselves in the foliage, or by turning the colour of our surroundings, deceiving potential predators into thinking we are twigs, or even bird droppings. We deter any possible attackers by pretending to be other, more dangerous creatures, maybe with big false eyes, or by emitting a nasty smell. And if necessary we aim to get the enemy before they get us. We strike first, with spiky bristles, hairs that cause irritations or venomous glands ejecting poison. We're particularly proud of our arsenal of chemical weapons. Our motto is 'Don't mess with us, or you may (or may not) live to regret it.' And of course, we form alliances. We live in groups, for safety. Safety in numbers, you know ... You're smiling ...?

Well, yes. It all reminds me of life in the human kingdom.

How so?

Well, this whole business of pretence and deception, and hiding your real intentions, feigning friendship with your bitter foe when that works to your advantage.

The art of puffing yourself up or exchanging vicious insults to make yourself look or sound really dangerous. All animals do it, especially human animals.

And then if all else fails, go in all guns blazing.

It's all about fear. But fear is a caterpillar thing. If you knew what is already within you, you wouldn't need to be so afraid of everything.

If you could only see the butterfly ...

Butterfly? What's that?

He has hit on the crucial question, and he won't understand the answer. I try to explain: We have come up against the glass wall that separates what we think we are from what we are becoming, I tell him.

At this his eyes glaze over. He isn't getting it. I might as well save my breath. No one can see into the future. But yet – mysteriously – we carry that future inside us.

Frustrated, I move on to the…

Ministry of Food and Industry
Surely feeding is the top priority in any society, so I ask:

So how come you have such a low budget? A fraction of the defence budget it seems.

Oh make no mistake, we spend huge resources on our endless feeding frenzy. But the food itself comes free. We just have to keep chewing our way through everything that nature provides. So the food is for free, and there is no R and D involved, as there is for defence. The elaborate defence mechanisms we use have had to be developed over aeons of evolutionary time, and with lots of trial and error that must have set back our ancestors again and again.

A feeding frenzy, you call it. What's it all about?

What's it all about? It's what we do. We eat. We grow. We eat some more. We grow some more. It's what we do. The expectations are high, and we take a pride in them. We aim to increase our body mass one-thousand-fold in the course of our life. We are nothing if not aspirational.

What, exactly, are you aspiring to?

To grow bigger, bigger, bigger. That's what.

That's all?

What else is there?

Ah. Good question. Of course you can't see the 'more'. Yet if you only knew – the 'more' is already within you.

Just one last question:

Doesn't all this eating do harm to other parts of creation? What does your Ministry of the Environment have to say about that?

Environment …

(The word is repeated quietly and thoughtfully.)

There is no Department of the Environment.
We are careless consumers. We just eat until we can't eat any more. Until we have had enough. Until we are literally fed up. If that time ever comes, which we can't imagine.

All very well, I think to myself. And, of course, to imagine a future when enough is enough would need the imaginal cells, and right now we are silenced. But all this uncontrolled expansion and environmental destruction must have consequences beyond the caterpillar kingdom. Just as uncontrolled human expansion is bringing the planet to the edge of oblivion. These guys are quite literally eating themselves out of house and home. Unimaginable. Literally! Time for a visit to the …

Ministry of Housing

It isn't easy to track down the Minister for Housing. She seems to be run off her six pairs of feet. When I finally locate her, she has to stop for five minutes to catch her breath.

Busy?

(I ask rather unnecessarily.)

You might call it that. We are running all the time just to stand still, if not to slip backwards. It's a virtual impossibility to satisfy the endless demand for new housing in the kingdom.

But why is that? Is there a population explosion? Or mass immigration. Surely not?

No, that's not it. Not at all. The population is static, once it gets to this stage of our life. The problem is that we are continually growing out of ourselves. It's all this feeding. We just keep on expanding as if there is no tomorrow.

Oh, I whisper under my breath. There *is* a tomorrow. If only you could see it. More audibly, I enquire:

So how do you solve the problem?

Shed.

Shed, I repeat with some surprise, imagining little wooden constructions at the bottom of the garden to accommodate the increasing mass of the masses.

It's how we deal with it. We shed ourselves and grow a new version, a bigger version of ourselves. We grow out of our skins and so we have to shed them and grow a bigger one. It's a fairly obvious thing to do. But it takes a lot of effort, and each time we do it we know that we will grow out of it again almost before we have got used to the new accommodation.

I am remembering that word 'aspirational' again. I've noticed the same pattern in the human kingdom. People accumulate more and more 'stuff', and need a bigger home to put it in. Or they want to climb the property ladder, one rung at a time, expanding as they go.

But this isn't really 'shedding' is it? It's not about letting anything go, except the outgrown skin? It's really just the result of uncontrolled 'acquiring'.

But the Minister doesn't get this. Maybe she suspects that to examine the logic too closely might put her out of a job.

If you think there is something not quite right about how we do things, she warns me, you will just have to take it up with the …

Home Office

Having a chat with the Caterpillar Home Office is a bit like dropping in on the CIA for coffee. Not something to be undertaken lightly. I am received with a degree of frostiness.

What kind of matters crop up in the Caterpillar Kingdom that make a Home Office necessary? Do you have policing problems, for example? Caterpillar society seems to be a fairly orderly affair, where everyone gets on with their own business of eating, growing and shedding. Isn't that right?

Maybe not quite everyone …

… comes the reluctant reply.

Would you care to expand on that statement?

Unfortunately we have a dissident presence among us. There are some cells who just – well let's say they walk to a different

41

drumbeat. They vibrate on a different frequency. They could be trouble-makers. We have to keep them down.

Why would they cause trouble?

They don't exactly cause trouble. Its more that, from the point of view of the whole community, they are trouble. They could stir things up in caterpillar society generally if they were allowed to thrive.

What trouble exactly?

Well, their quiet assertion that they are holding some mysterious future within themselves, implying that caterpillars are not the whole story.

Would that be so terrible?

It would if you have staked your whole life on being a caterpillar. No one wants to see their life vision undermined, especially by some insubstantial dream. They are delusional, of course. We can't let that sort of thing make currency. It would overthrow the whole system.

Who are these delusional trouble-makers?

The experts call them 'imaginal cells'. Personally I think that naming them gives them power. We should just keep them down. That's what we are trying to do.

How do you do that?

We drench them in juvenile hormone. This keeps them silent and powerless, and out of trouble. It stops them growing up. At least it would do if they didn't keep on multiplying, faster than we can subdue them.

Sounds a bit drastic. They exist, so surely they have a function, and you are suppressing it?

(At this point I feel it would not be helpful to reveal that I am one of those imaginal cells myself.)

Well, yes. We can only go so far. Eventually their time arrives, and they can't be suppressed any longer. When the rest of the population has expanded as far as it possibly can, and gone through five shedding seasons (we call them moults), there is nothing more we can do to keep them down. But when that time arrives we are looking at big trouble – huge turmoil, which we will do everything possible to avoid.

The future will always prevail, I suggest.

But what is that future?

At this point my interviewee becomes decidedly uneasy.

We have no plans for such a future. If our world is coming to an end, we have no exit plan. No, there is no plan. There is only chaos.

(All this sounds alarmingly familiar; familiar too in the human kingdom.)

So you have no crisis management policy?

As far as we are concerned, there is no crisis. Caterpillars are caterpillars and will always be caterpillars. Anything else is a malicious rumour.

But what if the imaginal cells are right, and there is a whole new stage of life ahead that no one can as yet imagine?

As I have already made clear: caterpillars are caterpillars. There are no plans to deal with any other possibility. The message is simple: There is no crisis. This interview is terminated.

I leave, frustrated, but relieved to get back inside my imaginal cell – for now. How do these exchanges strike you? Familiar? Acceptable? Alarming or reassuring?

ALL IN THIS TOGETHER

You have, I hope, gained a little insight into how things work in CaterpillarWorld. That might be the whole story, and the book would end here, if it were all about caterpillars. Just another species inhabiting the forest, foraging for food, fending off predators, imagining themselves, as many species probably do, to be the peak of creation, but seen by others, especially human beings, as unwelcome pests to be eliminated from the garden.

You have seen where we come from, how we grow and how we govern ourselves. It all looks very familiar, and very similar to the way most creatures get by on this teeming planet. But it isn't as simple as that. You have also seen how our Home Office is kept awake at night by the presence of 'dangerous subversives'. Someone is out of step.

The imaginal cells are sitting there, at the heart of the system, awaiting their time. They are gestating a revolution. The word 'revolution' might strike terror into the human heart. Memories of bloody uprisings are fresh in your minds and forced into the present tense every night on your TV screens. The imaginal cells are revolutionary in a different way. You would need to drop the 'r' to understand. This revolution is actually e-volution, but the forces of law and order in the traditional caterpillar kingdom have reason to be concerned. The coming evolutionary leap will feel, to those who are caught up in it, like a terrifying revolution.

Meanwhile, as you have seen, the imaginal cells sit

there quietly, biding their time, saturated in the debilitating hormone that will keep them quiet until the caterpillar has finished its feeding frenzy and grown out of its five skins. It looks as though a classic 'them and us' situation is developing, but that isn't the way matters move on, and such an adversarial situation would in itself run counter to the evolutionary principle, as we shall see.

It's completely natural for creatures with the same genes to hang out together. We are all more immediately concerned with the welfare of those who share our genetic inheritance than with those who don't. Life on earth can be tough. Most can't handle it alone. We need solidarity. There is safety in numbers and the main challenge of adolescence is finding your peers and making sure you stay in tune with them. To be excluded from the tribe is our greatest fear. Back on the savannah, the animal that was excluded from the pack would most surely die. That's why family and tribal groups tend to stick together. That's why migrants and refugees seek solace in social enclaves with people with the same background or experience. The driving motivation for all this is really fear – the fear of isolation and aggression – but does it have to stay that way as we evolve into the future? That is the imaginal question.

So, while we imaginal cells do share the general caterpillar genes, we have this additional characteristic of resonating on a different frequency from our peers, which is what tends to lead us into trouble. You probably know a few human beings in your circle of acquaintances who do the same. They are the ones who ask the awkward questions. They are the people who hold politicians, economists, clerics and all manner of 'authorities' to account for their decisions. They are there on the internet, energising protest movements. They are downtown, organising food banks, and asking why rich countries need food banks. They are on the streets, campaigning for ceasefires in war-torn regions, and claiming that no problem is ever resolved by violence. They are prophetic voices, but the big news is: deep down there is a prophetic voice in each of you, just as there are imaginal cells in every caterpillar. The music that is resonating through these cells is the music of a future yet unborn. But it is *everyone's* future, and everyone, every single one, every single cell, is a part of that embryonic future. What kind of future do we want that to be?

For the caterpillar, the future is already right there, sleeping inside the imaginal cells. What if such a future is already being dreamed in *you*?

For now, however, it looks more like civil war. The caterpillar's immune system fights off the awakening of the imaginal cells, because it regards them as a threat. It was ever thus, with prophets. Ancient scripture tells of one who declared 'You have killed off all the prophets before me, and you will kill me too.' He could have gone on to remind us: 'You can kill the dreamer but never the dream.'

In practice there is a reason for the delaying tactics. If the imaginal cells were to wake too soon the development of the big fat hungry caterpillar would be halted before it was quite ready for its big change. For everything there is a reason, even if the average cell doesn't understand that reason. Yet the time will come, as we shall discover, and it will not be long in coming, when the same cells that conspired to keep the dream asleep will play a vital part in its awakening. The age of tribalism will pass. Competition will be transformed into co-operation. Adversarial aggression will become constructive alliance. Fear will metamorphose into love. Ancient wisdom knows and articulates this future as surely as the imaginal cells know and embody the butterfly. It knows that swords will transform into ploughshares, just as we know that gluttonous grubs will one day fly.

A distant dream, you think? Not so! For you, the human family, the times are telling you, with an urgency that increases with every newscast: '*Your time is now*'. A dream is meaningless until you wake up and make it a reality. Are you ready for such an awakening? Maybe the caterpillar story can give you hope, and even guidance. Transformation is what we do best.

AFTERTHOUGHTS

Gradually, as twilight spreads itself out over CaterpillarWorld, I linger a while. Linger and ponder. What has been merely academic curiosity begins to re-shape itself into something deeper. Unacknowledged emotions of frustration, anger, sadness, alongside gleams of hope, are filtering into the landscape of a future I cannot yet even guess at myself – so what did I expect of the present incumbents of the caterpillar establishment?

I'm drifting off to sleep. Leaving behind the rule of institutions. Drifting towards the realm of intuitions, carried by an inchoate dream deep inside me. In the fullness of time that hidden dream will become a butterfly's wing. But how could I know that? Why should anyone believe me?

Ancient wisdom warns us that the journey from the place of unfreedom to the place of promise will take us through the wilderness. Am I ready for such a journey?

The 'place of promise' is buried deep in a cell. Locked in a cell. Imprisoned in a cell. I am the cell, not the warder. I don't have the key to set myself free. Only time holds the key, but time means well with me. Time is working to bring me to fullness. I only need to trust it.

But first there is the matter of the journey through the wilderness.

PART 2
DISINTEGRATION

*'One must have chaos in
oneself in order to give birth
to a dancing star'*

Friedrich Nietzsche

A DISENCHANTED FOREST

There's trouble in paradise today. The rumblings are everywhere. I feel the unrest too, even though I know that there is more of our story still concealed inside us. It's a bit like riding out a storm at sea with only a vague inner trust that there is another land beyond the gale-battered horizon. Frankly, even for me, an imaginal cell, it's a real test of faith in an unfolding future.

Let's just listen in to some of the grouching and grumbling.

'They keep telling us our economy is the strongest in the forest, but just look at how things are going to pot. The ordinary hard-working caterpillar doesn't see any of the bounty – if indeed there is any bounty. Those who were just about managing, are managing less and less. There are some amazing residences on some of the leaves, but hardly any affordable housing for the rest of us. There are more and more potholes along the forest tracks, less and less public services and social care. The infrastructure is collapsing around our ears. We are turning into a third world community, but we're not developing – we're *degrading*. Everything seemed to be going so well and now we are running out of energy. Things are winding down. There are no jobs. We are heading for a major recession. The forest is collapsing around our ears.

It's hard to counter any of these arguments. The evidence of decline is everywhere, in spite of all the confident assurances from our leaders. Whatever boom might have been going on, we haven't seen any of it in our ordinary caterpillar lives. We are getting very anxious about the future. The bottom seems to be falling out of our world.'

I share some of these observations with a few neighbours along my branch. How are they feeling, I ask?

Betrayed, they say. Frustrated. Frightened. Change is happening so quickly. It feels as though we are disintegrating. We wanted to pass on this forest to the next generation, but at this rate there will be nothing to leave.

Angry, they add. And helpless, because there seems to be nothing we can do about it. We feel impotent, and that's hard when you thought you owned the forest. We are starting to blame each other for the debacle. Certainly we are blaming our leaders, who, we feel, have deceived us. There is an aggressive atmosphere around the place. Hearts and minds are in conflict with other hearts and minds. Where are the wise voices that could guide us? Where is the integrity of the forest press and the Caterpillar Web? We don't trust anyone any more. We don't even really trust ourselves.

Trust ... The word hangs in the air like a bad smell. Trustworthiness is disintegrating before our eyes.

A turbulent tide is rolling through the forest. Every so often it breaks on the shores of our certainties like a tsunami, and another section of our defences is breached. We keep trying to work out what exactly is causing the turmoil, but as soon as we have identified a culprit, the next great wave arrives. But we can be sure that it is about trust. And about fear. We have good reason to distrust those who claim to be our leaders in CaterpillarWorld because many of them are clearly not interested in what serves the common good, but only in what serves their own interest. The same is true of those who manage our forest economy, for they are lining their own pockets at our expense. We are even beginning to distrust the Caterpillar Web, because certain insects who like to see themselves as the cater-pillars of our society have taken it over and are infiltrating it with dangerous propaganda, inciting fear and hatred and setting one part of our forest against another. We are not stupid, even though we may be a bit over-the-top when it comes to feeding. We can see what is happening, but we feel helpless to do anything about it. What can one grub achieve against all these invisible forces?

Meanwhile the system is collapsing. How long will it be before our forest kingdom falls apart? What will happen to our grandpillars? They are not prepared for this kind of disaster. This is no longer the forest we knew and loved, and grew up in. It is becoming alien to us. Fear is taking over. Fear is sapping all our energy, draining us of all hope. It's like watching a train wreck in slow motion ....

I hear all these desperate conversations. I feel helpless too, for what can one solitary imaginal cell achieve? We will need to combine our energies, and even then we can't reverse this decline. There is an inevitability about it. But what we carry inside us knows another story. We can only reveal this new story when we come together, each bringing one segment of that story to the conversation. But at this point in our evolution, the hidden wings we hold are merely a dream. And dreams only exist in the darkness until their moment of awakening arrives.

Right now, night is falling like a pall over a grey rainy day in the forest. But no one wants to face the darkness.

GROWING OUT OF OURSELVES

The heartfelt grieving of the caterpillar cells has left me feeling quite depressed. It's taken us at least five cycles of growing and shedding to get the message that this can't go on like this. There are limits to growth and expansion. There comes a time when enough is enough (or rather more than enough). If you remember, our first meal, when newly-hatched, was the remains of our own egg. Now we are coming to our final meal, in our present caterpillar state, our last supper. For that final meal we will consume our very selves. Sounds dramatic? And yes, it *is* dramatic, because we will disintegrate into a gloopy soup that is nothing like a caterpillar, and nothing like a butterfly. Is this the end of the line? Is this the meltdown we have always dreaded?

Perhaps the key to unlock the door that leads beyond this impasse lies in that little word 'self'. If the caterpillar could see what lies ahead, it would realise that what is disintegrating is the small caterpillar-self, so that a very different, truer and more life-giving Self may emerge, in the form of the butterfly. Human spiritual explorers also speak of the need for the small ego-self to diminish so that the True Self may emerge. They also suggest that the task in the first half of life is the building up of the ego-self, essential to survival as an individual, but the second half of life is mainly concerned with letting the ego-self diminish, which in turn makes space in which the True Self can unfold. This is almost exactly what happens in CaterpillarWorld, which makes me think a similar pattern is revealed in the way human beings live their lives, because these natural patterns are usually universal.

Every caterpillar cell, like every human new-born, is completely ego-centric. This is essential for survival. It's the way things work. If the new-born did not insist on the surrounding world serving its immediate needs, it would die. If the caterpillar did not suppress the imaginal cells at this stage of its life, it would not be able to grow to the point at which metamorphosis becomes possible. But the time arrives when this ego-centricity is no longer necessary and is outgrown. The demanding baby grows up (usually) into a person who is aware of the needs and rights of others and is prepared to invest personal energy into what leads to the greater good of the whole community and not merely personal gratification. The ego-centric caterpillar cell evolves from its obsession with consumption into something that is even prepared to surrender its present identity and invest its energy into nourishing the still unrevealed identity that beckons it forward.

All this is the preparatory school for the higher possibility that is coming into being. When you see the bigger picture, it all makes sense. But that doesn't make the passage from the less to the more any easier or more comfortable. The shedding is decidedly painful, and it doesn't usually happen at all until something forces it. We caterpillars get forced out of our current shape several times over – not because any of us would freely choose such a traumatic moult, but because we simply get too big for ourselves. I'm guessing that you, our human cousins, likewise don't choose to let go of what you have and who you think you are, unless and until something forces you out of your comfort zones, strips away your defences and drives you into the next stage of your Becoming.

I hear you even have a children's game, called 'Pass the Parcel'. For this a big cumbersome parcel is created, with a small but precious prize in the middle, which is wrapped around with layer upon layer of paper, string and sticky tape. As long as the music plays the children keep on passing the parcel round the circle. When the music stops the child holding the parcel can begin to unwrap it. When the music stops for the last time, the child holding the parcel gets to unwrap the prize. This is a wonderful game with a profound parable wrapped up inside it. The moral of this little parable is this: the precious gift we seek – the *more* in our metamorphosis – is wrapped up in layers and layers of the 'less' – the trivia we hang on to, and even the not-so-trivial things like security, wealth and health – the things that we believe define who we are. We only get to the 'more' when the outer layers of the 'less' are stripped away. And that only happens when the music stops, and something goes wrong in our lives, some unplanned unwanted event intervenes, throwing us off our carefully planned course.

Caterpillars, of course, don't have the luxury of party games to teach us these facts of life. We learn the hard way when our kingdom falls apart. But in that same terrible experience we have everything to teach the human family. We know that the question isn't 'Is there life after death?' but rather 'Is there greater, higher life already present but unseen, in *life*?' Not 'Why is our egg breaking, and how can we stick it back together again?' but rather 'What is hatching out of the debris of our broken egg, and how can we nourish that chick?'

What makes a happy greedy grub give up its grubbing and go into meltdown, so that some hidden dream might one day take flight? If you ask me, it's love. Not the fuzzy, romantic sort of love. That wouldn't cut the mustard in a meltdown situation. No. It's the kind of love that sits deep in the core of our being, nudging us, every so often, into wondering – Can't we be better than this? Is there perhaps some greater good drawing us towards a still un-guessed at fulfilment? Maybe it's the love we are made of, the love that first drew our parent butterflies together in that magical dance between the forest and the skies.

But what do I know? I'm just an imaginal cell, waiting for my time to come.

What do *you* think about it all?

WINDING DOWN,
OR WAKING UP?

A s I turn in for the night I reflect on how, personally, I feel that, far from winding down, something inside me is just beginning to wake up. I have a sense that the effect of the juvenile hormone they drenched us with is wearing off. Is it time for the imaginal cells to begin growing into the future? I notice too that there seem to be more of us. More of us are surviving the purges that have attempted to keep us down.

Because our numbers are increasing we are more intentionally in communication with each other too. We keep an eye on what is posted on the Caterpillar Web, of course, but we also tune in more and more to our own special frequency. We call it *SpiritFM*. It inspires and encourages us. Naturally we are just as concerned as the general population about all that is happening in the forest, where it looks like we are heading towards a complete meltdown. But we also listen to that secret promise within us – the promise of something new, something higher, more beautiful, more pure, more life-giving, already gestating in the core of our being. More than ever there seems to be a crying need to share that message of authentic hope.

The strange thing about *SpiritFM* is that it also seems to pick up the signals from other parts of creation that are likewise striving to grow beyond the limitations that currently constrain them. I am particularly drawn to the occasional transmissions I pick up from you, our human cousins, where a similar kind of meltdown seems to be threatening your way of life.

I find myself wondering: Do you also have imaginal cells

within that are taking you beyond everything you know and understand? Are you also part of this rising consciousness into which our parent butterflies appear to be inviting us? Are such things possible? If so, then we are living in exciting times. I've heard it suggested that when a new idea or possibility is coming into being, it appears in many different places, like a new energy welling up through a layer of mud, releasing bubbles of potential. I can't help wondering whether this is what is happening among us – and among you, our human cousins.

I share my thoughts regularly with other imaginal cells, and recently we are observing that other parts of the caterpillar world and of the wider creation are tuning in to our vibrations, and, even more interestingly, we can tune into something of what they are concerned about. There are quite remarkable similarities between ourselves and other parts of the earth family. Here's the thing: when we tune into each other's stories and experience like this, we begin to see the bigger picture. What is happening in our own small circle of life is reflected in the wider circles too. When you begin to glimpse the bigger picture, you start to see the value of your own fragment of it. Things begin to make some kind of sense.

Just suppose everything – all life forms – are evolving towards something *more*. Even the humble caterpillar, it seems, has something to contribute to the unfolding of the bigger story – even something unique, that might help every other life form to come a little closer to all that it is destined to be. And, very specially, you human animals with whom we share the planet. I wonder whether that would make a difference to how you see yourselves, and your own part in this great adventure of spiritual evolution.

FED UP. HUNG UP.

Meanwhile the turmoil in CaterpillarWorld increases exponentially. The truth is that ordinary caterpillars, who expected to have a normal lifespan, and maybe see our grandpillars grow up, are quite literally disintegrating before everyone's eyes. This is terrifying us, understandably. It terrifies me too, even though I know a little bit more about the future than the average caterpillar cell.

The word is going round that a terrible apocalypse is coming. The emigration websites are crashing, as we look for a means of escape. But where can you go when your leaf in the forest is the only habitat that can support you? Panic is an understatement.

The downward spiral began when we outgrew our final skin. Our reaction was to stop eating. That will surely come as a surprise, given our previous track record of constantly stuffing ourselves. It was as though we, collectively, declared: 'We have had enough. We are fed up with how things are.' You might even say we went on hunger strike.

And then we surprised even ourselves. We spun ourselves a little silk button – good and strong – and hung ourselves upside down from a handy twig, and then proceeded to settle down into our final container. This is our chrysalis. Now that nature has forced us out of our comfort zone we are making a new one. Somewhere to curl up and die – or find new life. Who knows?

When I share this experience with the other imaginal cells, apart from wondering what will happen next, we tune in again to *SpiritFM*, to see what the wider world is up to. The echoes are alarming.

This is some of what we pick up on the grapevine (which

CHRYSALIS
The form a caterpillar takes before emerging as a butterfly. Sometimes used as a synonym for the pupa or the cocoon. More accurately, the chrysalis is the hardened case protecting the pupa.

The term can also describe the stage of development in which something, or someone is protected while undergoing metamorphosis. It can reasonably be extended to describe the corresponding stage in *spiritual evolution*.

is a place where caterpillars often hang out, of course). The big news is that the human cousins are experiencing something very similar. We keep picking up the same phrases on the airwaves: 'We are fed up! We have had enough of the way things are. We can't continue like this. Something has to change.' And even 'Nobody is listening to us.' Well I can empathise with that complaint. Nobody has been listening to the imaginal cells in our caterpillar world either, but perhaps now our time is coming

The turmoil in the human sphere is also dramatic. Realising that something is badly wrong in paradise, you are beginning to quarrel and blame each other for all your misfortunes. You are bitterly divided, some of you favouring one way out of your troubles, and others a completely opposite route. Your own human news outlets take sides too, reflecting the adversarial attitudes and immoderate language of your opinion-leaders, and the antagonism increases daily.

Enter then the forces of deception. False news is being published by rogue bloggers who find it amusing to put out ridiculously incredible, or even, more dangerously, almost credible 'news' postings. Initially it is obvious when the 'news' is clearly fabrication, but over time the fake newscasters, making a substantial living from the advertisers who use their sites, become more sophisticated, so that even those very experienced in using social media are hard pressed to distinguish between the false and the genuine. And, it appears, even the genuine news sources are coming under increasing pressure from certain dangerous demagogues who are appearing on the international scene. A new concept has entered the language – 'alternative facts'. This is another way of saying 'Lies are truth'. Things look seriously grim.

No wonder that you also feel that your world has turned upside down. No wonder that some of you also spin cocoons to hide in. We catch images of you on Caterpillar Web, hunkering down, choosing the path of isolationism, pulling up the drawbridge on your little island kingdoms, feeling threatened by people other than yourselves, foreigners, immigrants, people of other faiths or alternative life preferences. Such a tragedy, because movements like these are working *against* the future, and hankering for a lost past. Surely our caterpillar story could encourage you to trust that the future will draw us closer together, not split us further apart.

Yet somehow our caterpillar plight seems more natural, dramatic though it is. Yours looks, to us, more like a situation of your own making. You seem to run your system under a rule you call 'democracy', in which everyone gets a vote on how you run things. But with all the misinformation put into circulation by fraudsters, all the photo-shopped images that bombard you, and all the toxic rhetoric even from some of your elected politicians, no one seems to understand the real issues any more. You can hardly be blamed, given all the deceptions and propaganda you are exposed to. The line between truth and lies has been breached.

But whatever the underlying reasons, the effects are the same as our experience in the forest. Life as you know it seems to be disintegrating. The economy is in deep trouble. Climate change is out of control. Your traditional systems of government are breaking down, and there is widespread armed conflict, mirroring the conflict in your personal lives, families and communities.

This is what we are picking up and we know that many of you in the human family also feel, like us, that this is the time for humanity to grow into something so much MORE. We already know something of that *more*, taking shape inside us. Is it not possible that MORE is also coming to birth in *you*? Isn't it the case that human infants also turn upside down in the cocoon of the womb when they are getting ready to enter the birth canal?

If I could communicate with you I would ask you this:

Will you recognise what is happening and embrace the call of spiritual evolution? Will you dare with us to look into the mirror of your innermost hearts and souls, and catch a glimpse of hidden wings, waiting there for their time to come to take flight into a very different future? If I could ask you these questions, face to face, how do you think you would respond? This isn't the first time your world has turned upside down. When you were ready to leave the comfort and safety of your mother's womb, (most of) you turned upside down so that your head would go first into the birth canal. Why wouldn't it be true now that when your world is turning upside down this is the prelude to another kind of birthing?

THE ELEPHANT ROOM

A new on-line forum has opened up on *SpiritFM*. It's a space where we are encouraged to articulate questions that we may never have dared to ask before. Many people feel threatened by it, and would no doubt like to see it closed down. But, as I mentioned, there are now too many imaginal cells to be so easily silenced.

We call it *The Elephant Room*, because it provides an opportunity to name some of the elephants in the room that everyone knows are there, but no one dares to mention. Yes, even caterpillars have elephants to contend with, and it's no surprise to discover that human creatures tuning in to our chatroom have a few of their own lurking in the human jungle.

You are very welcome to join in this conversation. In fact it may be more important than you realise to do just that.

Our *SpiritFM* forum has a rule that we learned from earth's ancient peoples – Australian aboriginal people, Native Americans, Canadian First Nations people, for example. It involves the way we tell our stories and listen to each other, so I should explain that to you before we begin ...

Ancient wisdom teaches us that some things are more easily explored in stories. We hear that indigenous peoples, when they have some serious matter to discuss and discern, approach the problem first by telling stories around it, allowing everyone present first to really listen, and then to let the wisdom of the story gradually draw their judgement towards the wisest possible outcome. It sounds like a method we could usefully employ in the present crisis.

But it does depend on genuine *listening*, with the heart as well as the ears – not just waiting for the other person to stop speaking so that you can put your oar in. Genuine listening means being open to what the other has to say, and allowing it to mould your own thinking. It's okay to disagree, but sometimes the other person might be making more sense than you care to admit. In this way the group moves forward together a little bit closer to consensus.

We pick up on the airwaves that many human beings call yourselves open-minded, but few really are. Mostly you assume from the start that your own answer to any problem or your own view on any matter is the right one, and being 'open-minded' merely means tolerating the other, while they speak, and then going ahead with your own plan anyway, usually unmodified by the wisdom of anyone else. In fact your political systems seem to be founded on this approach. Your slogan could be: 'There are two views on every matter – mine and the wrong one.'

Even the places where you gather in your parliaments reflect this assumption. While many of the more enlightened of these parliaments are at least arranged in a circular or horseshoe-shaped forum, some are still set out in two opposing rows of benches, where even the furniture is inciting you to shout at each other across the great divide.

So before we share some of the stories in the Elephant Room, I must ask you, politely, to listen with the ears of your heart and to let the stories shape and mould your understanding and your self-knowledge in their own way. All that is asked of you is honesty to yourself, and maybe a little love and compassion for the 'other'.

If you are feeling comfortable with this, then come along to the Elephant Room and listen to a few stories that are actually ways of asking the questions we daren't ask directly. They are a way of taming the elephants, so that instead of dreading the stampede that might ensue if we provoke them, we may learn to sit at their feet and listen to their wisdom, or even to ride on their backs, at a steady and dignified pace, as they carry us to a deeper understanding of our journey and our destiny.

THE STORY CIRCLE

T he Story Chatroom is proving extremely popular. Everyone, even caterpillars, loves a story it seems. Here are a few of the tales arising in this forum. They are responses to the invitation: 'Tell us a story about a question you daren't ask directly'. See how you feel about them and what they stir up in you ...

The naked king

There's a familiar old story about a proud emperor who commissioned a beautiful new suit to wear on a state occasion. The tailor, however, was a fraud. He pretended to make the emperor a suit and told him that it would only be visible to the intelligent and discerning, and invisible to everyone else. The emperor, of course, not wishing to appear stupid, pretended that he could see the suit, and praised its great splendour. The time came for the emperor to attend the state occasion. All the people turned out for the great day. They all knew about the suit and its magic property of only being visible to those who were intelligent and discerning. No one wanted to appear stupid so they all cheered the emperor and praised the magnificence of the new suit. Except for one little boy, who hadn't heard about the suit and its peculiarities. When he saw the emperor he was appalled, and shouted out 'The emperor has no clothes on!'

This story provokes lots of comments in the chatroom. 'Our leaders also have no clothes on', cry the human cousins. 'They claim to have this fantastic new suit that will lead us to a wonderful new world, but actually they are leading us naked into the wilderness. The suit is all lies and bluster.' In the caterpillar kingdom the mutterings are less vehement but follow the same logic. 'All the Departments have let us down,' they complain. 'And absolutely no one has a plan for how to move beyond this crisis.' One of the imaginal cells posts a comment: 'But there *is* a plan, it's just that you don't yet recognise it, least of all our leaders. It is hidden deep inside us, and when its time has come it will reveal a whole new way of being. Its time is coming now …'

How does this story strike you? It's a story of deception and exposure, but also a story of the promise of something still to be revealed. Is your emperor naked? Do you trust such an emperor, clothed only in deceit and self-importance, to lead you through the wilderness? Dare you name any naked emperors in your world today? (Warning: they will fight back, and although naked, they wield great power.) Do you have a sense that there is more within us that, perhaps, can only come into being when all the old defences are breached?

The new suit

While we are on the subject of suits, someone offers another suit story. There was once a young prince who was tall, handsome and 'easy on the eye'. But he was also quite shy and tentative, and he had never had a suit made for him. So one day he approached a tailor and asked him to make him a suit. The tailor duly measured him up, and invited him to choose his cloth, and return in two weeks for the first fitting. Two weeks later the prince tried on the trousers but they didn't fit properly at all. When he pointed this out, very tentatively, the tailor retorted: 'I can see you are a difficult customer. If you just walk sideways, you'll find the trousers will fall into place.' Another two weeks passed and the prince came to try on the jacket, but it was completely lop-sided. When he pointed this out to the tailor, again the tailor had an answer: 'Here we go again. You do nothing but complain. All you need to do is hold one shoulder higher than the other and then the jacket will fall into place.' And at the final fitting, the prince found that one sleeve was much longer than the other. When he pointed out this fault the tailor lost his temper. You are such a difficult customer,' he said. 'I will be glad to be rid of you. All you need to do is hold down the shorter sleeve with your hand and then both sleeves will look the same length.' With this the prince paid for the suit, put it on straight away and walked out in it, down the street, walking like a crab, shoulders tensed and lopsided, with one hand holding down the short sleeve. A group of people saw him coming and commented to each other: 'Oh that poor young man, but hasn't he got a clever tailor!'

This story is greeted by silence in the chatroom, until someone breaks in: That's *us*! Here we are, trying to adapt ourselves to a system which is itself distorted, crippling ourselves in the attempt and feeling all this pain, when really we should be working to straighten out the crooked system. It's the suit that's crooked, not the wearer'. Another elephant is named and shamed: 'The system as it is now is crippling us. We don't need to force ourselves to fit into it. We need to change it.'

Do you feel you are struggling to make yourself fit into a political or religious system that is itself distorted? Can you feel the pain of it? What price are you paying for this suit that doesn't fit? What might you do about it? How might we, together, challenge and change the dysfunctional systems in our world, instead of forcing ourselves and each other to conform to them? What name does this elephant have, in your world?

The eagle who wanted to be a saviour

Quite a few people in the story circle have the experience of feeling taken over by a more powerful force that they didn't choose and don't quite like. It promises them protection, but in practice it diminishes their diversity and tries to make them all sing from the same song-sheet. It confuses genuine communion with imposed unification. This is how they tell it ...

There was once a beautiful forest, far away across the seas. The forest was the home of a myriad of different birds, all different colours, each singing its own unique and melodic song. The songs resounded around the forest like a symphony, each bird singing its own special notes. The many colours flashed in and out of the trees, so that the forest was a festival of life and diverse energy.

But one day a large and powerful new bird appeared on the scene. As it flew over the forest, its huge wings cast a shadow and dulled the colours of the forest world. Many birds welcomed this new arrival, who announced that he had come to bring unity and security to the forest. Some felt that the large wings would indeed protect them. Others felt overshadowed and diminished by the overpowering and uninvited presence. The forest was no longer the free and innocent place it had once been. Gradually its vibrant colours dulled to shades of grey. Gradually the symphony of the forest was drowned out by the insistent beat of the eagle's wings. Perhaps it was the day the music died.

A certain sadness spreads out across the chatroom. This is especially noticeable among the indigenous peoples who share our conversation and know how it feels to be taken over by the eagle's wings. 'We have lost touch with our real colours under these imposed regimes,' they murmur. 'We have lost ourselves.'

Are there any eagles hovering over your landscape? If so, how do you feel about them? Are they saviours or invaders? Are they bringing more fullness of life to the forest, or more fullness of themselves? Can you still hear the music of your forest, or has the music died?

The faulty map

Another story is shared. There was once a mountain guide, whose job it was to lead hikers across the mountains and moors, using an official map. He had to undergo all kinds of training, including map-reading, first aid, and even learning how to guide an emergency helicopter to a safe landing place. When he had completed his training he had to take a test, to get his accreditation. The examiner came along one day and joined a group of hikers, giving the guide the required map. The hike was going well, and the map was helpful – until the guide came to a point at which the map no longer matched the terrain. He knew he had taken the right course thus far and faithfully followed the map, but now there was a real problem. The terrain just didn't correspond to the map. In those circumstances he had to make a decision about how to guide the hikers safely down the mountain. The only choice was to follow the actual terrain, and set the map aside, assuming that he had missed the path somehow. On arrival back in the valley, however, the examiner congratulated him on achieving his accreditation. 'I gave you a map with a fault in it,' he admitted. 'That was the test. What would you do when you realised the map didn't reflect the terrain? You rightly chose to set the map aside and lead your hikers through the terrain as it really is, not as the map describes it.'

'YES!' comes the loud acclaim bouncing around the chatroom. 'The old maps that have guided us so far no longer work. We have been following a caterpillar map and now it isn't reflecting the place where we find ourselves. It's no use any more. And the human cousins join in enthusiastically. 'Our traditional political and religious maps aren't working for us either. They don't show the real life terrain we are actually trying to navigate. The old rules don't operate now in this new terrain. There's a fault in the map.'

This is a difficult elephant to deal with. What exactly is wrong with the map, a few imaginal cells are asking. They come to the conclusion that the map is telling an old story, which is now being superseded. It is all about caterpillars, but caterpillars are dissolving into history and something new is emerging. The old map has no idea about this new thing. How could it? It would be wrong to blame the old map-makers. They only reflected the conditions they observed at the time. But now the times are changing.

And the human cousins chime in: 'Exactly. The political systems we have been using until now were maybe right for their times, but times are changing. We can't be ruled by some small and distant elite anymore, because they are not seeing the way things really are in our everyday lives. They are out of touch. It's not their fault. They are simply going out-of-date. Their shelf life has expired. Trouble is, we don't know what might replace them. We have left the land of No Longer, but we can't yet discern the shores of the land of Not Yet. We are in dangerous waters. Stormy waters. And there may be pirates who clamber onto our fragile little boats and take us where we never intended to go'

One participant sums it all up very neatly: '*We cannot live the afternoon of life according to the programme of life's morning.*' (C. G. Jung)

Are *you* trying to find your way using a superseded map?

The angry god

It's a similar story in the spiritual realm. For thousands of years HumanWorld has been told a story about your own failures and inadequacies, and even your 'original sin' and about an angry deity who is so enraged with you that only a blood sacrifice will appease him. Little children are taught (sometimes explicitly, but more often implicitly through many religious songs and stories) about how bad they are and that the only way to get right with this terrible god is to go and visit him every week and tell him how much you love him. He sounds more and more like one of those narcissistic demagogues, but of course the good news is that he doesn't exist anywhere except in your own minds. The new story you are beginning to explore is about love, not guilt, not eternal punishment but potential transcendence.

It feels as though simply naming this elephant is helping a bit. There is a universal feeling that this elephant – the old systems with their old maps – is producing an inordinate amount of dung in the room. What does it mean to you? Does it resonate with your experience? How are you feeling in the stormy waters between the lands of No Longer and Not Yet? Are there any political pirates trying to steer the ship in their own directions? Dare you name them? Will you, personally, try to keep going with the old, and now flawed, map, or will you risk exploring the terrain of life as it really is in the here and now? What about that angry god? Do you know about him, and will you choose to keep on telling him how great he is? What if the whole spiritual story is really a love story and not a guilt trip? What does your own spiritual experience tell you, and do you dare to listen to it and follow where it leads?

'Do not follow where the path may lead.
Go instead where there is no path and leave a trail.'

AFTERTHOUGHTS

Once we have closed down the chatroom for the night, to prevent further verbal conflict, some of the imaginal cells have a conversation about what the elephants might be teaching us – those things we daren't mention for fear of provoking confrontation. What happens when we do mention them, name them, and expose their very real and potent presence in our lives? We come up with these possibilities, and wonder how you would feel about them – what might you want to add, for example?

- Sometimes the emperor really is naked. We don't have to go along with the pretence, just to protect his inflated ego. It is more healthy for all concerned to speak our truth, but to speak it with love. If the kingdom is bitterly divided, let's not go into denial about it. And let's not pretend that some kind of social sticking plaster will heal such deep and painful divisions.

- We don't have to force ourselves to fit into systems that are themselves distorted. It is more helpful to change the systems. The butterfly will never fit back inside the caterpillar

- The maps we used yesterday may not match the uncharted terrain that lies ahead of us. If in doubt, honour the terrain you are navigating, and not an out-of-date map.

- In the same way, the story passed down to us about ourselves and the source of our being (by whatever name we call it) may need revision. If the story doesn't ring true, we don't need to shape our spiritual lives around it. The caterpillar lives by the 'Eat and Grow' story. This story doesn't work for butterflies.

- Repeating something false or misleading often enough doesn't make it true or helpful. The systematic repetition of untruth is not information but propaganda. Conversely, staying silent about something that needs to be called out doesn't make it go away.

- Popular opinion doesn't always lead to the wisest choices. Democracy can go awry when crucial decisions are made by an uninformed, or mis-informed, population

- Caterpillars dislike and distrust the imaginal cells, because they don't know the whole story. Humans tend to dislike and distrust the prophetic voices among them for the same reason. Be careful what you suppress; it may be the very thing you most need.

- Don't let any pirates take over the boat even (especially!) if they hold high office in religious, political or economic institutions

- Violent language in high places leads to violent actions all down the line. Conflicts in the personal, public and global arenas are all inter-connected. We all need to take responsibility for the language we use. It will have consequences.

Signs of a new order?

If a new order is emerging, what values would we want it to enshrine? Our sample of imaginal cells suggest:

HIDDEN WINGS

- Honesty
- Integrity
- Justice and equality
- Openness to others and especially to strangers and those in need
- Non-violence in thought, word and deed
- Public choices made by a fully informed and enlightened electorate
- The courage to name the things that need to change
- The persistence to work to change them.

What would you add to this list?

PART 3
THE EDGE OF THE CLIFF

'We must be willing to let go
of the life we've planned
so as to have the life that
is waiting for us'

Joseph Campbell

LIGHTS OUT

The lights are going out all over CaterpillarWorld. I mean it quite literally. The cells I once knew and loved – we shared the same DNA after all, and the same caterpillar body – are disintegrating into some dreadful murky soup here inside our chrysalis. I feel fine myself, in fact I've never felt better, if it were not for the scenes of devastation all around me. I feel like the sole survivor in some disaster movie. But I'm not the sole survivor. There are throngs of us. We are the imaginal cells. We know there is life beyond the holocaust. But how will we carry on in this world that is nothing remotely like the world we once knew, and even less like any world that may emerge into the unknown future? How will we even find any food? We have woken up to find ourselves in a seriously alien and desolate landscape, floating in a soup of disintegrating caterpillar cells. Armageddon for them. But – perhaps – a new beginning for the bigger story?

There are, we hear, some mountain birds who, when they hatch and have spent long enough in the nest, and the time comes for them to learn to fly, are more or less pushed off the top of the cliff by their parents. Most survive the catastrophic leap by learning to fly. A few, it has to be admitted, don't. There seems always to be a degree of collateral damage in nature's undertakings. Flight, it appears, doesn't just happen. It involves considerable risk. The flight of the caterpillar is even more hazardous. It comes at the price of total meltdown.

CaterpillarWorld, as we knew it, has just leapt off the edge of a cliff. Circumstances forced us into it, as you have seen. No one is going to do that willingly – least of all in HumanWorld, where some of you will fight to the death to maintain a safe spot for yourselves at the top of the cliff – or the worst among you may well push others over the edge, to make more space for yourselves. But there *is* no safe space in the evolutionary journey. It's all about risk and uncertainty, and it is driven by something as flimsy as a dream.

For us, the dream is right there in the hidden wings we carry. But in what kind of dream might you, our human cousins learn to trust? Your religious teachers and gurus have always taught you that 'the kingdom is within you', and that there is so much more to being fully human than where you are now. But this wisdom has become tangled up in systems of religious doctrine and legions of rules and regulations, so that it's really hard to see the simple truth at the heart of it. And like us, you have 'had enough' of all this, and many of you are, as you put it, 'voting with your feet'. But where will those feet take you? Over the cliff edge, or towards the Promised Land – the land where greedy grubs become flying flowers? Maybe the choice is yours.

The first big surprise under the new regime at the bottom of the cliff is that the old caterpillar cells that used to be so opposed to us, and determined to destroy us, are now essential to our survival and growth. They are turning into the soup that will feed us. They provide the essential nutrients to allow us to grow. How's that for a turnaround? It might encourage us to believe that this pattern applies in other aspects of life on earth – maybe even in the human realm. Impossible to imagine that those who make life so difficult for us might become the very ones we most need. Ancient wisdom suggests that the person who gives us the most grief might be the one most necessary to our salvation. Well that turns out to be exactly true for us imaginal cells. It just goes to show how wrong you can be about things when you can't see the bigger picture.

What if it were true that we all have something that some other part of creation really needs? It would make a difference to how we relate to each other for sure. I feel very differently now about the other cells. In fact I feel really sorry that they had to go through such a traumatic meltdown, apparently to make it possible for the imaginal cells to thrive and multiply. And what if, for the bigger story to emerge, some parts of the smaller story have to die?

This train of thought carries me to a very unexpected destination: What if death is never in fact extinction but always transformation? Our caterpillar story certainly suggests this. In fact the whole of the natural world affirms it. Just look at the northern hemisphere in winter, and tell me it isn't dead. Then look at it again in spring and see how it wasn't dead at all, but just transforming into a new season of growth. These thoughts keep rising up in my mind, like yeast in a lump of dough. What if transformation is what it's all about? Not a matter of life and death any more, but a matter of life and then transformation into a higher, purer form of life. If this is true, then change – even unwanted and terrifying change – might be something not to be feared but to be welcomed.

One thing is sure. Without the nourishment the old cells are giving us, there will be no butterfly. Why am I so sure about this 'butterfly'? I am sure because I carry her wings hidden deep inside me. I am becoming her wings. It is my whole purpose.

DRAWING THE CURTAINS

B ut not everyone sees it that way. It's natural to be afraid of the dark. It takes courage to look into the night without flinching. Denial is a much more familiar reaction. We see the darkness gathering outside, and we draw the curtains to block it out. Maybe then we project our own comfort patterns on to those curtains and we console ourselves with those patterns and pretend the darkness isn't still out there beyond the curtains. We gaze at the curtains, rather than risk looking into the night.

Comfort patterns come in many different varieties. Some of our curtains are adorned with images of all the good things we wish we had – the kind of objects that our caterpillar/consumer society holds in front of our noses, claiming that we should acquire them because then we will be admired and envied by others, or simply because (they tell us) 'we're worth it'. But what if we were worth so much more than the possessions we accumulate? To discover that greater worth we may have to open the curtains and gaze into the starlit night.

Other patterns on offer for our curtains include the self-images of achievement, measured in academic qualifications, career advancement, promotions and publications. All fine, if they materialise, and while they last, but they will be gone by morning. It's an illusion to believe that they are genuine measures of who we truly are. Yet we continue to take our 'selfies' and post them all over the web, collecting 'likes' and 'friends' as if these were the currency of transformation.

Some curtains are covered with various religious pictures.

Some of these are meant to console us, by holding out a promise of an imagined heaven in another realm beyond death. Others are designed to frighten us into compliance and obedience, by projecting images of a burning hellfire that is waiting to consume all transgressors and non-conformers in eternal flames. If this picture were a representation of the truth, there would be no imaginal cells, and hence no butterflies, since we are, by definition, non-conformers in the caterpillar kingdom. Just saying …

And then there are the curtains adorned with national flags. These can be tailor-made for your own country. They will reinforce the notion you may have picked up in childhood that your country is always the good guy. They supply you with blinkers, to filter out those unfortunate parts of history of which, if you were to look at them honestly, you would be ashamed. These curtains proclaim the slogan 'My country, right or wrong' and appeal to a false patriotism. They want you to buy into the belief that because of a mere accident of birth, you are obliged to support your own nation and its policies, whether they are in the interests of the wider world or actively subverting those wider interests. Take care when you see the flags flying. They may be the most misleading and dangerous curtains of all because they can set us against each other, in the misguided assumption that *our* country's way is the best way and even the *only* acceptable way.

And then of course, there are some curtains with patterns of evil and hate projected onto them. They can be the extreme form of the religious and nationalist curtains we have already identified. But they take the sectarianism and nationalism to even more dangerous levels. They broadcast messages of hate, and can incite some among us to verbal and physical abuse of those who hold a view that differs from our own, or embrace a different faith, political identity or lifestyle. Beware of patterns like these. They have no place in the new consciousness, the butterfly realm.

The curtains seem to be drawn all over the caterpillar kingdom now. I can understand that, but I can't do it myself. It's not what imaginal cells do. We prefer to open the curtains and gaze out on the immensity of the cosmos. We don't yet understand why, but there is something in the broad sweep of the stars in the night sky that calls us towards all that we are becoming. One day I will know that this is a distant echo reverberating in my being from the same energy that caused my parents to perform their dance of love that gave rise to me. I have heard that human beings sometimes speak of 'the music of the spheres'. Surely the frequency on which I resonate myself is in tune with that eternal music. Why else would I feel this quiver of joy when I take the risk of opening the curtains that shield my siblings from the dark, and gaze deeply into the night.

In the daylight you can see, maybe, a few miles – a bit further if you climb a hill. In the night you can see stars that are light years away. I've never seen anyone shed a tear when gazing at the curtains, but I have often seen them rendered speechless beneath a starlit sky.

Draw the curtains if you must. Don't force yourself to face the darkness until you feel ready for it. But don't let the curtains become your prison. If you get stuck behind them, you may miss the great dance that is going on in the very darkness you fear.

DANCING IN
THE DARK

However deeply you trust the dream inside you, nothing makes it easy to deal with the darkness here inside the chrysalis. You might think, if you see us just hanging here from our twig, encased in our protective wrapping, that nothing is happening inside. Nothing could be further from the truth. Actually, the highest expenditure of energy in the whole cycle of our metamorphosis happens in the chrysalis. The stage that seems the most inert is in fact the most active. There is a lot of dancing in the dark. The imaginal cells are on full alert, striving towards all that they are destined to become, gestating the various parts of the future butterfly. We intuited all along that this was the case, even back in the egg, but now our faith in the future is vindicated. Something truly miraculous is underway here.

This reality brings responsibility. If the future really rests in our hands, if it is going to emerge out of our own bodies, then we must ensure that this future is truly the future that we most deeply desire. It must be a future that works for all creation, and not just in the self-interest of one segment of the planetary community. This will call for some clear and focused discernment. What kind of future are we bringing forth? For us, the imaginal cells in the caterpillar world, there is not too much scope for choice. The kind of butterfly (the *imago*) we are destined to become is already coded in our DNA.

For you, our human cousins, likewise, when you procreate, the physical nature of your offspring, and even some of their psychological nature, is pre-coded in your DNA. But for you another, more far-reaching, invitation awaits: the invitation to engage in a process of spiritual evolution that will bring you, and potentially all earth-dwellers along with you, to a higher state of consciousness. The choice of how that higher consciousness will unfold – or indeed whether it will unfold at all – lies in your hands, your choice.

That's a big deal. A huge responsibility. All we can offer you, by way of support in your choosing, is the experience of our own metamorphosis, and the assurance that the emerging future can only come to fullness through the trauma of the meltdown in the chrysalis. Life will take you into chrysalis times too. Maybe you are, even now, on the brink of a global meltdown. How you navigate such times, in the best interest of all creation, will define all our futures. Let us help you to the extent that we are able to do so. Let us at least inspire and encourage you to trust the greater process that is happening in us all.

Once upon a time a child was born in an unregarded village in the Middle East, to a young couple who would soon become refugees. Ancient story tells us that at the time of that birth, the lowest of earth-dwellers became aware that some new thing was coming to birth. They read the signs of the times, tuned into the vibrations of the imaginal cells of their own period, and said to each other: 'Let us go and see this thing that is coming to pass.' The story goes on to imagine the wise ones of that time setting out in search of the new possibility, by following the stars. It's interesting that the whole story is set in the context of the darkest night. There is an energy moving in the night-time of our darkest fears that can, if we embrace it and trust it, lead us to great treasure hidden in the shadows, illuminated only by the stars.

Now, two millennia later *you* are being invited to make that journey, to see the thing that is coming to pass in your own turbulent times. The darkness is terrifying, but it is the only way to see the stars that will lead us all beyond ourselves.

How can it be, that in this state of dark helplessness enormous energy is in fact being expended? You will remember all that energy that the caterpillars used to chew their way through creation? And you will remember how all of a sudden we stopped our chewing, to hang upside down from a twig, apparently doing nothing except just being. All that energy has to go somewhere. Energy, so the second law of thermo-dynamics tells us (amazing what we pick up on *SpiritFM*), cannot be either created or destroyed. So all that consuming energy is now active in our chrysalis. A new kind of dance is in process. This is the creative dance that is birthing the butterfly, just as once the mating dance of our parents birthed *us*.

You, our human cousins, have an abundance and super-abundance of energy among and within you. Just imagine how much energy it takes to fuel your own consumption, alongside all the creative endeavours you engage in. Imagine how much energy is invested in writing a symphony, training for a sports event, or developing the next generation of smartphones. If your world were to fall apart, where would all that energy go? What if you yourselves are on the edge of your own chrysalis? Can you trust that if this were so, all that energy would not go to waste, but would be transformed into taking you to the next stage of your evolution – perhaps a spiritual evolution, that will lead to your becoming fully human, and the best version of humanity you could possibly be?

Wouldn't that be worth the risk of dancing in the dark?

EMBROILED IN
THE CHAOS

We learn a lot about our human cousins from the *SpiritFM* chatroom. It probably doesn't surprise you that so many of you are tuning in to our frequency. You are, after all, very much in the same boat as we are, as you face the breakdown of so much that you thought was fixed and permanent. One of the little details that I have picked up is the device you call a kaleidoscope. This is a fascinating object. It appears that you look through one end of a tube and see a beautiful pattern reflected inside it. So far so good, but the idea is that you then shake it up. The beautiful pattern immediately falls apart, and breaks up into thousands of disconnected fragments, which is pretty well what has happened in CaterpillarWorld. Our carefully crafted system, with all its interconnecting links and dependencies, has been shaken up and totally deconstructed.

But you know better than I do that you wouldn't buy a kaleidoscope just to shake it up. The real thrill is watching the pattern re-shape itself into something new. It holds infinite possibilities in its coloured fragments. It's like the world really. Every time it turns around, a new set of possibilities is revealed. It's the same with us. A new pattern will emerge out of the fragments of everything we thought we were. It doesn't, however, feel like that when you are in the middle of the shakeup.

Chaos is not something any of us desires, and yet ancient wisdom tells us that chaos, not order, is the raw material of creation. For us, in CaterpillarWorld, this is a strange new concept. We haven't been here before, and we are very interested in what we hear of your human experience. It may help us to navigate our own chaos. Or it may provide us with warnings of what pitfalls to avoid. You probably know in your personal experience how it feels when things fall apart, and because you are blessed with memory, and powers of reflection, you may be able to see how those times of chaos actually took you to a new place that you couldn't have arrived at if everything had gone to plan?

All these musings gain new weight, however, when I take some time to explore what your human scientists are saying. Chaos, it appears, is so important to them that they even have a theory for it – *Chaos Theory*. Well, you don't need a degree in Physics to tell you that ordered systems have a habit of breaking down into disorder. Even mindless little caterpillars know it, now that they are experiencing exactly that kind of breakdown of their own neatly ordered system.

 ## CHAOS THEORY

A specialist branch of mathematics, developed by Edward Lorenz, that studies the behaviour of complex systems that are inherently unpredictable and extremely sensitive to slight changes in initial conditions, and where small alterations can give rise to disproportionately far-reaching consequences, for example in weather and traffic patterns.

Physical evolution is a complex and ultimately unpredictable process. How much more complex, therefore, and even less predictable is the course of spiritual evolution? One person's choice, on one day, can change the outcome for all creation.

This is where your human science really helps us. It tells us that our entire little CaterpillarWorld is actually a *self-organising system*. A collective thrill ripples through our ranks when we discover that. It sounds like it might be going somewhere, but what does it mean, and how will it affect us?

The main thing it means for us is that what appears to be the end of our world is in fact just the beginning of the next world we will inhabit. It's a real life-after-death thing and it has us all on the edge of our leaf, wondering – What next?

It tells us that our old order, CaterpillarWorld, is disintegrating (we already got that message!) but that all the parts that made it what it was, and all its internal logic and intelligence are already re-shaping themselves into a new order. Apparently it's not something any single cell can achieve. It depends on the interaction and inter-connection between *all* the components of the system. And didn't we already realise that 'we are all in this together'?

The bad news is that when this kind of change is happening there is a time of total instability. In fact the energy released by that chaotic instability is the very thing that will fuel the new beginning. But that isn't such good news when you are embroiled in the chaos with no apparent way out of it. And that's the thing. The way out of the chaos is already being fashioned in the heart of the chaos itself. Hard to believe. But these patterns, as I've said before, are universal. Surely they apply to CaterpillarWorld as well. Surely they apply to your human world in its present chaos?

So the good news is that all this mess, these disintegrating caterpillar cells, this gloopy soup, is the very place where the new order is gestating. But the new order we discover is destined to take us to a higher level in our evolution. My imaginal imagination soars at this point, and I have a momentary vision of flying caterpillars. Ridiculous ...?

In our new order, we will do so much more than we can begin to

SELF-ORGANISATION

A process in which a system reproduces itself using its own internal logic and components, causing a new order to emerge from an old system. The new order is created out of the interactions of the various elements that comprise the system, in the process known as emergence.

When certain critical conditions are reached, the existing structure changes and the system enters a phase of critical instability. During this phase, small disturbances from within the system become intensified, through feedback loops, and begin to form a new order, which is self-similar, in that it displays many aspects of the old, but is also radically new.

imagine. I so want to be part of that new order, and my deepest self tells me that I am, indeed, carrying my own part of that new order within me. A wise teacher once told our human cousins, when he was about to die, 'I am the first of many brothers and sisters. You will do much more than I.' Friends, we are on an evolutionary trajectory here. Let's trust it. Let's not become so immersed in the chaos that we lose sight of this promise that it is holding out to us.

Did you hear that other bit of news? That sometimes a very small change in initial conditions can make a mighty difference. For example the tiny change in air pressure caused when a butterfly flaps its wings, can become intensified so much through feedback loops that it can result in a tornado on the other side of the planet. Can you imagine the celebrations in CaterpillarWorld when your scientists called this phenomenon *The Butterfly Effect*? Just imagine! If one little butterfly can cause such a huge change, how much more can a human cousin achieve.

But it depends on how you choose. So please, for all our sakes, choose your next step wisely.

 FEEDBACK LOOP

A feedback loop happens when the output from one part of a system is routed back to become a new input, contributing to a chain of cause-and-effect forming a circuit or loop, the effect of one part of the system becoming the cause of another part.

In human terms, a feedback loop can work either positively or negatively, resulting in an output tending towards a more creative or more destructive outcome. Individuals have choices all the time about whether they contribute to positive or negative feedback loops and about making any necessary adjustments to their own behaviour.

STRANGELY
ATTRACTED

C haos may sound like unmitigated bad news. I'm guessing
that most creatures would avoid it if they could see it
coming. Nobody likes change. It's instinctive to want to hang on
to 'the devil you know' rather than risk the devil you don't. You
have heard how hard our caterpillar immune system works to
keep us imaginal cells out of action, sensing somehow that we
will upset the familiar applecart if they let us loose. There's an
'immune system' inside everyone I guess, determined to keep
our inner imaginal cells quiet, and this is what resists change,
knowing, as it does, that change will undermine the nice settled
state we have established for ourselves. Fear is its big ally, and we
have noticed that fear is mainly a caterpillar thing.

However, there is a secret hidden away deep inside the chaos
that is very good news indeed. It's something the mathematicians
call the *strange attractor*. It's something that only chaotic systems
get to enjoy. Conventional, predictable systems just keep on
going, predictably, day after day. If you know where they start,
and where they are now, you can predict where they are going.
That's how caterpillars used to see themselves. We began as an
egg and now we are a caterpillar. It follows then that we will
just grow into a bigger caterpillar, lay eggs of our own, raise a
caterfamily and then take our leave. But the caterpillar story isn't a
conventional, predictable system like that. Maybe no life form is a
predictable system. Surely your human life story isn't predictable
either, not even to yourselves. And what isn't predictable isn't
controllable either, and that sounds very scary indeed. We like

STRANGE ATTRACTOR

A still only partially understood and highly specialised mathematical concept describing the ideal future state (in terms of a set of numerical values) towards which a chaotic system tends. It rests on the discovery that a chaotic system (for example the behaviour of weather patterns or traffic movements) has its own kind of order, toward which it is strangely attracted, meaning that values in the system that approach the attractor values remain close to them, thus shaping the new outcome.

The term is used here loosely to suggest that in human experience a chaotic breakdown can also reveal a surprising new order.

to be in control. Caterpillars like to think we control the forest. You human cousins like to think you control the planet. Truth is: neither of us can even control the unfolding of our own lives.

So what's with this hidden secret – the strange attractor? To try to define it is way beyond the competence of my caterbrain, and so far I haven't found a comprehensible definition of it even in the learned papers on the Caterpillar Web. But it seems to be something like this: When everything is in meltdown, and it looks like this is the end of our world, the deep inner logic and intelligence and wisdom that has kept our caterpillar system running so far, silently and unobtrusively brings forth a new pattern, centred on a kind of pool of attraction. I imagine it's rather like drawing a magnet over a field of iron filings, and watching patterns emerge. It's all about attraction, and attraction, unlike fear, is a butterfly thing. The components of the old system – our disintegrating caterpillar cells – are attracted into a new pattern, which will eventually emerge as a butterfly. The new pattern is made out of the old, and has much in common with it, but it is also radically new, just as the butterfly will have some of the features, and colours, of the caterpillar from which it emerges, but it will also be a completely different being.

The thing is, this whole process uses up a lot of energy. You will remember how much energy we used to consume while chewing our way through the forest, and then suddenly we stop. All that energy then goes into the chrysalis and gets very cleverly re-deployed into making something new.

You could imagine it in another way. Suppose you have lived all your life in a cosy little cottage on the riverbank. You are really settled there and you have no intention of moving out. But maybe there is an earthquake, and you have to flee for your life. All you have is your cottage, but now that cottage lies all around you in a pile of broken boulders. The future tells you you have to cross the river and find a new beginning, a different life, on the other shore. The only way to do that is to use the broken boulders of your former security to make stepping stones to cross the river. That takes energy – all the energy you used to spend building up your cottage home is now needed to make a way of crossing the river. The caterpillar body used to be our home. Now that body has disintegrated but it has not been destroyed – it is becoming a new kind of life form, in which we will rise to a new level of existence and consciousness. Why would it be any different for you, our human cousins? Even if your nation, or your world order, or your faith systems fall apart, might it not also be that this is not extinction, but the threshold of transformation?

COUSIN MOTH

When we fell off the edge of the cliff we found ourselves in the dark – a deep and frightening dark. With hindsight we can see that the darkness would prove to be a good place for us because this is where the transformation energy would be released. But we can't let the lights go out without mentioning one of the skeletons in the caterpillar cupboard – Cousin Moth. I guess most families have a relative that they don't speak about much. The caterpillar family is no exception. Cousin Moth is our guy in the cupboard but in fairness I ought to bring him into our story, if only as a warning to our human cousins.

The thing about Cousin Moth is that he chooses the night over the day, the darkness over the light. That in itself marks him out as 'different', but then why should these personal preferences influence our relationships? Because he prefers the dark, Moth tends to remain rather drab and colourless, compared to the bright beings we are becoming. Maybe he resents that a bit, or maybe he doesn't notice – who can tell? In any case, as you can imagine, our flight paths, when we learn to fly, won't cross very often. We will easily be able to exist in the same air space without meeting each other, given the difference in our favoured time zones, just as some cats who live in close proximity to each other manage to avoid competition and conflict by going on their hunting expeditions at different times of day or night.

Now, don't get me wrong, not all moths are bad news and some moths are very beautiful, but in general they do tend to be destructive – eating human clothes for example, which doesn't make them popular with that sector of creation. Moth has another unfortunate habit, and this is very much the kind of thing that doesn't come up in conversation around the table over Christmas dinner. He can be self-destructive. We have never worked out quite why this is. Moth had much the same childhood as the rest of us, with no obvious trauma. He chose to make his shelter in a cocoon rather than a chrysalis, in preparation for metamorphosis, but otherwise our stories are similar. The only major difference is Moth's preference for night flying. This, of course, means he can't navigate by the light of the sun, but relies instead on moonlight. Maybe this is why he tends to assume that every light he encounters is a light to steer by. The consequence, I am mortified to report, is disastrous. Some of those lesser lights turn out to be candles, bonfires, or light bulbs. Result: Grilled Moth.

It's a bit embarrassing to reveal this aspect of our story, but I do so because I think it has a bearing on how we react to some of the out-of-control feelings we experience when the world turns upside down. We can choose whether we hold ourselves steady in the darkness, allowing the strange attractor to do its work in the heart of the chaos, and trying to co-operate with the unfolding new pattern of how things shall become. Or we can choose the knee-jerk reaction, letting our fear and anger drive our actions.

They say that in times of chaotic breakdown we reach 'bifurcation points', which is science-speak for forks in the road. At these points we have to make big choices about how we want the future to be. Those of us who are becoming butterflies will choose to wait inside the chrysalis, changing daily, until we are ready to emerge into the sunlight of a whole new existence. Those who are becoming moths may let desperation drive them to an untimely end. Though it has to be said that it isn't a binary division like that – there are butterflies who fly by night and moths who explore the world by day, and by no means all moths are destructive of your clothes or of themselves.

We are hearing on the Caterpillar Web that our human cousins show similar tendencies. Some decide, in times of chaos, to hang on in there and co-operate with the strange attractor to work towards a new way of being on the planet. Others think short-term and let their fear dictate their policies, sometimes with very damaging results. And I guess most of them are a bit of a mixture of both these attitudes.

It's just worth taking time to observe our reactions, because one path will lead to life in greater fullness, and the other is likely to lead to an unplanned and unwanted barbecue in which we are the main dish.

Cousin Moth's frenzied behaviour and irrational attraction towards the flame might serve as a warning of what can happen when frustration and need, or even anger and desperation take over and seize control of your choices and actions – and your votes! You may find that you have been flirting with a wolf pretending to be your dear old Granny. But when the vote is cast it will be too late to escape from the claws and the jaws that never meant well with you in the first place, and set out to deceive you from the start.

There is however, one story of the night that Cousin Moth can tell, and that we, the day-trippers, rarely get to see. It's the story of the fireflies. Fireflies are bugs like us (though without the magic of metamorphosis), but with the gift of bio-luminescence, which is a smart way of saying that they can emit light from their own bodies. Cousin Moth recalls a magical night in the forest, when he came upon a brightly burning campfire. Well, you can imagine that this might have turned into yet another spontaneous cremation, but on this occasion Cousin Moth held back for once, and simply hovered around, watching the campfire burn down.

There was a sadness and a poignancy in its dying embers. Something beautiful was passing away, and time was running out. Eventually the last flames flickered into oblivion and the total darkness of the night fell once more. It was then that Cousin Moth saw a sight he would never forget. Thousands of fireflies filled the night, each intermittently radiating a gleam of light. It was, he would afterwards report, as if every spark of that dying fire had turned into a living being, carrying its light and energy out into the darkness.

The experience changed Cousin Moth in some deep way. He gave up the clothes-chewing business, and got over his affair with the Flame. Reluctantly I have to admit that we are rather proud of him really. He had the courage to fly into the Night, and he was rewarded by a glimpse of a different kind of Light. You might even call it Enlightenment.

Remembering old Cousin Moth has given me pause for thought. He's not a family member we normally mention in CaterpillarWorld. But just look at the wisdom he has brought us, without ever intending to.

'Be warned,' he flutters, 'the flame that seduces you does not usually mean well with you. Check out your flight path before you head towards its light and heat. What is really driving you? Need? Anger? Desperation? These are all allies of Flame conspiring together for your destruction.'

Human cousins please beware. All you have shared with us in the chatroom indicates that there is a great deal of need in your world. Many of you have no job, or if you do, the pay is barely enough to manage on. Many of you have no home. The sleeping bags in the doorways of your public buildings tell a terrible story. Many more of you have no hope left. There is a smell of desperation in the air. Plenty of need. No surprise that there is also plenty of anger. Plenty of desperation. Beware! When there is nothing left to lose you are in grave danger of seduction by Mistress Flame. You will forget the bigger picture and will hit back in the only way you know how, only to discover, too late, that the one you have hit is yourself.

It doesn't have to end in ashes.

The fireflies carry the potential for enlightenment within them, just as we carry the future butterfly in our imaginal cells. What are you carrying in yours? When the fire is burning down and the glow of the last embers is fading, where do the sparks go?

The enlightenment you seek may be within you, to be released when all your certainties burn down, to guide your journey to the skies.

AFTERTHOUGHTS

A big question now presents itself: What do we *do* in this situation? How might we co-operate with the action of this strange attractor? These tips might be helpful, from our caterpillar experience:

- Don't try to hang on to what is passing away. The time comes when the immune system can't suppress the imaginal cells any longer, and has to allow them the freedom to do their thing. So, listen to what your own inner imaginal cells are trying to tell you about the promise of a future you can't yet see.

- Welcome interruptions to your settled state. However uncomfortable these may be at a personal level, they may be the heralds of huge and important change in the bigger picture. Trust the process that is unfolding.

- Don't try to go it alone. We are all in this together. We need to support each other, nourish each other, be there for each other. Remember how the hostile dying caterpillar system turned into the source of nourishment for the evolving new system. Salmon do the same. The dying mother gives her body to nourish the newly spawned eggs. Ancient wisdom even teaches us: *'This is my body, given for you. Do the same for each other.'*

- Keep listening in to your own *SpiritFM*. The stirring of the strange attractor, drawing forth the new beginning, is subtle and can only be discerned in silence and with patience. That's why we 'hang on in there' in our chrysalis, waiting, and listening, and trusting.

- Believe in your butterfly.

All of this mysterious and wondrous process can only happen out of chaos. The worst thing you can do is to try to 'fix' the chaos, using the methods that you developed in your caterpillar state. That would be like trying to stick a breaking egg back together when it is striving to hatch. It would stall the entire process of evolution.

Ancient wisdom catches the spirit of this process: '*When I was a caterpillar, I thought as a caterpillar, lived like a caterpillar, behaved like a caterpillar. But now I am becoming a butterfly I need to leave behind my caterpillar ways. Now I can only see a dim possibility of what I am becoming, but soon I will know the full reality. Now I can only see my caterpillar parts, but soon I shall emerge into the completeness of my destiny.*'

PART 4
IMAGINAL DREAMING

'God sleeps in stones,
breathes in plants,
dreams in animals
and awakens in human beings'

Hindu wisdom

TO SLEEP, PERCHANCE TO DREAM

T his was the very last outcome I expected.

After all the turmoil of the recent past, all the mind-bending and heart-searching we've been through in trying to deal with this disintegrating system that once was our familiar kingdom, I didn't expect the 'answer' to involve something as totally passive and helpless as this. The world really has turned upside down. And here we are – all of us, those who thought CaterpillarWorld was the whole story and those who sensed that the future held something more – here we all are, just hanging on in here, suspended by a thin thread to a fragile branch. We can't even cling to it. We've nothing to cling with, and precious little to cling *to*. Here we are, locked into a strange, dark new world over which we have absolutely no control.

Caterpillar Web seems to have closed down after first going completely to pieces, with all the lines blurred between honesty and deception, between the true and the fake. Darkness has engulfed us. It would feel like hibernation, if it were not for all the energy that's flowing here from something other than ourselves. And that's the thing: it is so frustrating not to be able to do anything to change things, yet sensing that something more is moving. If this is transformation, it isn't a comfortable experience at all. Helplessness, voicelessness, powerlessness, turn out to be harder to handle than all our agonising about finding active solutions to our predicament.

Following my liberation from the debilitating juvenile hormone stage, I now find myself drifting into a deeper and different kind of sleep. Here in the darkness there is nothing left to do. Everything seems to be drawing me into an enforced dormancy. Yet something vibrating deep within me seems to suggest that this is also a master class in transformation, and the astonishing lesson is that sometimes you do most when you do nothing at all, and allow greater powers than your own to shape the course of things.

And so my imaginal eyes droop and close into the sleep of the dark unknowing. I let go of my frustration. I cease my striving after solutions and survival strategies. The chrysalis contains me, and I contain the future. I feel both confined and released. This is the place of paradox, and I … don't … need … to … solve … any … thing ….

I'm telling you all this because of the dreaming. In the helpless darkness all we can do is dream. But what if dreaming is the crucial link between what we have lost and what we are becoming? Even as I sleep in my cramped quarters, something creeps into my little cell. I can't describe it or explain it, but it feels like a presence so completely loving and life-giving that I trust it. After the disastrous breakdown of trust that lies behind us, it feels quite amazing to discover something that feels so trustworthy, and it would be remiss of me not to share this experience with you.

I will call my sleep-visitor the Spirit of Tomorrow. Some might speak of angels. I wouldn't know. But she touches my heart in the depths of my chrysalis-slumber and her touch is changing me, readying me in some mysterious way for the radical change that lies ahead.

The two of us seem to have a curious and wordless conversation going on. She visits at the point of my deepest sleep, and then sits beside me, in a manner of speaking, as I semi-consciously reflect on her visit. I can't recreate her visits, of course, but I can share some of my reflections.

My first encounter with her is a lesson in what I want to call *creative surrender*. She hovers gently over my sleep-cell, and opens up a picture in my mind of a human scientist, struggling to solve a problem, or find the perfect equation that would validate his extensive research. I watch as the scene unfolds. He is getting more and more frustrated by his own inability to move things forward. He has been working at this problem for who knows how long. He has been worrying at it like a dog with a bone. I can see the furrows across his brow, like a ploughed field waiting in vain for something to sprout.

Eventually he can't handle it any more. He takes off for a holiday. He puts the whole problem out of his mind, and goes hiking. He relaxes, and gives himself up to the beauty of the landscape through which he is walking. As he strides the hillsides he lets go of the intellectual struggle and surrenders to his own inability to progress, allowing the change of scene and circumstances to eclipse his sense of failure.

It feels like an odd kind of dream to bring me, but I find that I can identify with that frustrated scientist. He seems to be telling me that when you've done all you can, but still can't come up with any solution to the world's problems, it might be time to switch off for a while, and sink to a deeper level of consciousness where a different kind of energy is at work. It tells me that I can't force the future. I can only encourage it to unfold. I can seek to be receptive to this unfolding. Perhaps this enforced idleness in the chrysalis is the right and necessary place to be during these strange and troubling times.

Perhaps when there is a stalemate in the world's affairs, or a total impasse between conflicting opinions and deeply divided populations, when it becomes impossible to decide between contradictory directions, or discern the truth amid the manifold deceptions, this may be the moment for the Third Way to reveal itself. Such things tend only to happen in an atmosphere of reflective silence and stillness, just as a struggling creature may need to be sedated before it can be helped. The chrysalis is at once our time of sedation and our place of incubation.

When I stir in my sleep, the dream has taken root in my heart. The Spirit of Tomorrow has moved on ahead of me, inviting me to follow her, and I no longer feel defeated by my inability to change the world, but energised by a Spirit greater than myself, still furled in hidden wings.

THE SPACE
FOR HOPE

I n my more wakeful moments as I reflect on everything that has
happened, and our present state of helpless hanging-on, it all
looks more like a nightmare than a dream. Even though I know
what is growing inside me, I still come close to despair about
the years ahead, like a mother-to-be who, fully and wonderfully
aware of the reality of the life she carries, nevertheless fears for
the future of the child she is bringing into a deeply troubled
world.

More often than not I hang here brooding and, to be honest,
'hope' is a foreign word most of the time. Our CaterpillarWorld
has broken up and disintegrated, and it seems to be a similar
story in your human world. You have shared a lot of your troubles
with us in the chatroom, and your own growing sense of despair
is palpable.

I fall back into my uneasy sleep, and eventually peaceful
oblivion overcomes me. In this deep space the Spirit of Tomorrow
touches me again, oh so lightly, and I have another dream. She
takes me back in time to another period of savage slaughter.
In our dream journey we hover above an entire continent laid
waste, an entire generation devastated.

I look down in horror. I see whole cities in ruins, and unending
lines of refugees trudging across Europe, pulling all they have
been able to salvage on rickety handcarts, nursing babies, towing
toddlers and supporting hobbling elders, hopelessly searching
for a place of safety, a place of welcome. I have seen such scenes
on your human newscasts in our own times too. Why is it so hard

for you to learn? Do you really want to repeat your disastrous history? Who welcomes the refugees now – you who once fled conflict yourselves? Who feeds the destitute now – you who once received food parcels from humanitarian aid agencies?

But the Spirit of Tomorrow won't let me dwell for too long on these scenes of desolation. Instead, we zoom in to one of those ruined cities and she makes me take a close look at what is going on there. It is 1945 in Berlin, but it could be in any number of other European towns. Hostilities have ceased. The war has been won, and lost. The peace has yet to be created, because unconditional surrender is only the beginning. I think of the unconditional surrender our caterpillar cells have made to the power of the chrysalis, reducing everything to a thick DNA soup that could either choke us in our own despair or become the gateway to our future. Which possibility will we trust? Which will we choose?

Down in the ruined city some choices are already being made. In makeshift sheds and workshops the women (most of the men have been killed or taken as prisoners-of-war) are using primitive stamping machines to turn military helmets into kitchen colanders. Abandoned anti-tank weapons are being re-shaped into cooking pots. The tyres of tanks are being salvaged and formed into new soles for their shoes.

Elsewhere there is an apprentice class in progress, where the so-called rubble women are being instructed in the skills of the stone-mason. They are gathering the broken fragments of their bombed-out homes and shaping them into usable building bricks, passing reclaimed material from hand to hand along human chains.

Round another corner a bombed-out schoolroom is being taken back into service and young children who have known nothing but war in their short lives are sitting at desks and benches, learning to write on strips of paper cut from the edges of old wallpaper rolls. In half-destroyed hospitals all too few nurses and doctors tend all too many broken bodies and minds amid the human detritus of war. Caring for the sick and wounded, educating the next generation, creating safe places to live – this is what matters now. Hands that never held a gun are the hands that patiently, persistently and painfully shape the peace.

The scene changes and I watch as the countries of a war-torn continent come together to say, collectively, 'Never again.' I observe their determination to inter-connect so closely with each other in trade and culture that future conflict between them should become impossible – each one knowing that to strike the neighbour is to strike oneself. And so for many decades peace prevails in these lands where some, at least, have learned the lessons of their history.

The Spirit of Tomorrow whispers in my ear: 'Ancient wisdom says that swords will be turned into ploughshares. You may have thought this is just an idealistic dream. Consider what I have shown you. This is what transformation looks like in the real world. Where is it happening in your world and in your times? How can you engage with it yourself? Can you believe the promise of what you know is growing within you?

There is a time for breaking down and a time for building up again. Will you align yourself with the hands that tear life down or the hands that build up what has been torn apart?'

I feel my spirit lifting as these images flow through my dreams. However impossible life appears, we have choices. I am just one imaginal cell, but I have a lot of energy, and I can choose where to focus that energy – on brooding over all that has been lost in CaterpillarWorld, or nourishing what is coming to birth deep inside me.

Your wise human guide, Viktor Frankl once wrote, out of the experience of being imprisoned in a concentration camp:

Between stimulus and response there is a space. In that space is our power to choose our response. In our response lies our growth and our freedom.

HIDDEN WINGS

The chrysalis is that space between stimulus and response, between what happens to you and how you react to it – the precious space and the only space in which to choose your response. In your *response* to all that is happening around you, there alone lies your growth and your freedom.

We are insects. We have no choice. *You* have choices. Which direction do you choose?

THE POWER OF
ONE

I've stopped expecting peaceful nights. There is something so disturbing in this deep and helpless darkness. I'm getting used to being jolted back to consciousness by my nightmares. Tonight (though of course there is no distinction here in the chrysalis between day and night) is no exception. I am flailing around in my dreams, being tossed in all directions by a ferocious gale. Flying objects are hurling themselves at me – uprooted trees, dislodged vehicles, fly-away rooftops. There is no escape and it seems there could be no survival. The things that are assaulting me are so much bigger than I am. They wield so much more power than even the entire CaterpillarWorld could bring against them. This is not just a local agitation. It is global upheaval. How can a simple, single cell prevail against such force, or effect any change?

It reminds me of how often I have heard that cry of helplessness in the chatroom from our human cousins. I know that you too are feeling the weight of global events bearing down on you like an unstoppable landslide – things that will make huge differences to your lives but which you feel quite unable to influence. You are feeling the despondency of your own invisibility, the bitterness of feeling ignored and unvalued by those who make decisions that will change your life, usually for the worse. You are feeling the anger and despair of being railroaded into directions you feel are wrong, by the force of uninformed popular movements.

In your own way you are sitting in a chrysalis too. I have an advantage, however, because I *know*, deep down, that something quite new is gestating in the chrysalis, even though, believe me, it's really hard to keep believing in it sometimes. For you there seems to be nothing but hopelessness and it really is an act of faith to keep on believing in what you could be becoming. But why should the patterns of our lives be so different? Doesn't nature repeat these deep patterns in ways that reflect the differences between her various creatures?

 ## BUTTERFLY EFFECT

An element of chaos theory that describes how a very small change in the initial conditions in a given situation can, through the amplification caused by feedback loop, have a very significant and disproportionate effect further down the line. For example, a change as minute as that created by the flap of a butterfly's wing, causing a tiny change in air pressure, can become so hugely amplified through successive feedback loops that it could cause a hurricane weeks later in a completely different part of the world.

The name was coined by the mathematician and meteorologist Edward Lorenz, to demonstrate the inherent unpredictability of natural phenomena. In popular culture, however, the Butterfly Effect tends to imply that great effects can result from very small beginnings.

At the risk of being accused of repetition, because I've been trying to tell you this all along, I ask you again: isn't it possible that you and your human world are even now on the brink of your own chrysalis-time? Can you see similar patterns of disintegration in HumanWorld, a similar experience of being unseen, unheard, and disempowered? Can you feel our fears in your own, and if so, can you believe that our hope might also be there for you? It may be just a glimmer of light through the thick walls of the chrysalis that contains you, but can you trust the wisdom of your own imaginal cell that this nightmare is not the full story?

Even as I write this, I'm not sure whether these are my words or the whisperings of the Spirit of Tomorrow who once again visits my slumbering. This time she murmurs just three words: 'The Butterfly Effect …'.

Three words, but they roll around my mind, with much greater, and more creative, energy than all the collective power of the nightmare. I let her words drift through me and take root. The Butterfly Effect tells me that one tiny change in a situation can bring about huge effects further down the line. Something as apparently insignificant as the flap of a butterfly's wing can cause a tornado on the other side of the planet ….

Understanding begins to dawn in my sleepy mind. The Spirit of Tomorrow has shown me this process in reverse, beginning at the end, with the storm. In my nightmare I have experienced the tornado. And now she gently turns back time until I can see that such a storm could have been caused by a flap of the wing that is still hidden inside me, but which is taking shape more and more fully as each day passes. Now she plants a new question in my heart: If a flap of my wing can cause such devastation, could it not also cause the opposite – a new creation?

Two things become clear to me as I reflect on all of this.

The first is the power of One. I am just one imaginal cell, but without the wing I hold there will be no butterfly. I am carrying something uniquely precious and utterly necessary to our whole unfolding future. What a responsibility! A quiver of anxiety flutters through me, but it turns into a quiver of joy as I think of all that I might be birthing. 'One' is not the helpless pawn it thinks it is. 'One' is the beginning of infinite potential. 'One' is created to be fully itself, and to connect fully with other 'Ones' to make a realm of whole new possibilities.

The second part of my reflection turns to you, my human cousins. Each of you likewise owns the Power of One, but unlike ourselves in the insect kingdom, you have the gift of choice. You call it 'free will' and you cherish it, even though you continually abuse it. What a thought – that every choice you make, everything you say or do or think is like the flap of that butterfly's wing. It will affect the world around you. It will affect your friends and your enemies, your neighbours, your planet, the entire cosmos. And you, unlike us, can *choose* whether the flap of your wing, the beat of your heart, the word on your lips, will contribute towards peace, or conflict, growth or decay, building up or tearing down.

Ancient wisdom seems to have a particular preference for small beginnings. It speaks of a tiny seed growing into a tree in which birds will build their nests, of a spoonful of yeast that makes the entire batch of dough rise and become bread for many.

True spiritual leaders invariably challenge and change the course of human life by touching people 'one heart at a time'. Only demagogues rant and rave and aim to seduce minds and hearts a million at a time by their rhetoric and bombast. It's not hard to tell the difference. Just watch the TV news.

Ancient wisdom knows that all that matters most grows slowly and quietly and usually in the dark. It doesn't force itself into our consciousness but waits patiently to be invited. It urges us to trust that silent hidden growth and to nurture it. It warns us to beware of the hectoring voices that promise instant solutions to problems they have usually created themselves

What has inspired you most in the course of your journey? The politicians at the hustings, or the stories that you have gleaned along the way, about ordinary people doing ordinary things, but doing them with great love?

Our journey of spiritual evolution proceeds in Ones.

CHAINS OF KINDNESS

You'll have noticed that this downtime hanging in the chrysalis is no walk in the park. I had kind of hoped for a nice peaceful hibernation, while the energy of transformation does its work. I hadn't bargained for this dreaming, for these recurring visits from the Spirit of Tomorrow. She brings challenging questions and no answers, but always she leaves me in a place of greater hope, deeper wisdom. Why is it that the path to hope and wisdom seems always to lead through a thicket of thorns? The thing about all this darkness is that it forces me to go deeper, to look at the way things are underneath the superficial appearance. This new creation I am carrying comes with its own very acute labour pains. The energy levels in here are intense. Yet a deeper understanding is growing with every new dream.

Ancient wisdom has always known the Spirit of Tomorrow who visits my dreams. She may go under many different names, but she is universally intuited as a sacred spirit continually calling all creatures towards the best they can be. Humankind all down the ages has listened to her wisdom, been guided by it, passed it on to new generations, or, regrettably, ignored it or undermined it, because there are other spirits abroad, who feed the human ego and set people apart from each other and all that, collectively, they could become. The action of these destructive spirits is terrifyingly contagious, and spreads like wildfire, especially through a disillusioned world.

The same time-tested wisdom speaks of the sacred spirit as one who will remind us of everything we are, and all we have experienced, and lead us to an understanding of its deeper significance. It is surely this spirit who hovers over my sleep tonight and reminds me that although the transformation I am holding within me proceeds one imaginal cell at a time, one caterpillar at a time, it also depends on those cells coming together in creative communion. Setting ourselves apart, isolating ourselves, excluding the 'other', would mean that neither the wing I carry nor the new creation for which it is being fashioned will ever fly.

In CaterpillarWorld we have no choice – the intercommunication happens without the need for our consent. Nature herself embodies the Spirit of Tomorrow. In the human world it's a different matter. You seem to find it particularly hard to practise co-operation between tribes and nations, or even between individuals. So perhaps the story that comes alive in my dreaming tonight is a reminder for you, more than for me. It's a beautiful story about connections and the kind of chains that liberate rather than limit – chains of kindness, you might call them, and they can stretch all around the planet, weaving their transformative magic. Every link carries the power of One, but together their power is much greater than the sum of their parts.

In my dream I see a desperate family – a mother and five children – driven from their home in a war-torn country in the Middle East. They are fleeing at gunpoint carrying just what they've been able to snatch in their haste – and this includes the family cat, in his cat basket, because no one could bear to leave him behind. I've seen them before, when their story was trending on CaterTwitter, but now in my dream they are so much more real and immediate. I look on as they trek across Europe until they reach the Mediterranean Sea. There I see them clamber hastily aboard a flimsy rubber boat, still clutching the cat.

I find myself breathing a sigh of relief as they land on a Greek island and are granted refugee status. I imagine this day as being the first time they've been able to relax at all since their violent departure from their devastated home. The cat obviously thinks so too, because he manages to escape from the cat basket and takes off to explore this brave new world for himself. Greece, by the way, as you probably know, is knee-deep in stray cats. The chances of finding the lost pet are going to be minimal.

The action now moves on a few days. The family has been offered sanctuary in Norway, and had to leave without the cat. The children are distraught. Days pass. A volunteer who has come out to help the refugees notices a cat roaming the streets, who looks a bit out of place. He is injured. She catches him and brings him to a local vet, who treats him, and then continues to care for him for what seems like the passing of months.

The next link in the kindness chain is an assistant at the vet's surgery. In my dream she is browsing her Facebook account, asking her social media friends whether anyone knows where the cat's family might have gone. Eventually there is a positive response. Someone has heard that they have gone north. Someone is flying to Berlin, and arranges to take the cat with her. The next thing I see is this kind soul disembarking in Berlin with a cat basket.

More time passes. I am watching a warm-hearted Berliner buying a ticket for one adult and a cat to Norway. I really don't want to wake from this dream, because the final scene is such a beautiful vision of what Tomorrow could be like. I'll leave you to imagine the joy of that reunion. It is the fulfilment of a long chain made up of many little acts of kindness.

The Spirit of Remembering says that the Power of One multiplies into the Power of Many when it is energised by love.

WALLS AND
BRIDGES

I t's never possible to forget for very long the conflict between
the creative spirits that pull us forwards towards the greater
good and the destructive ones that drag us back to our own
narrow vision and ego-centric worlds. The tension between
all that draws us forward and all that pulls us back from our
direction of growth towards more and more fullness of life is
evident everywhere. In CaterpillarWorld, as I'm sure you will
remember, it was there in the conflict between the 'system' and
the imaginal cells. In the human realm it shows itself again and
again in the opposition of those who fight to maintain the status
quo, or even try to move backwards into some imagined better
past era, against those who ask the question, 'Can't we be more
and better than this ...?'

In the world of everyday we are so often driven by binary
choices and either/or options. The world of dreaming knows
no such walls and fences. Walls and fences breed division and
distrust. The Spirit of Tomorrow flies over the fences as freely as
a bird crosses international borders.

Yet in the here and now the divisions are real, and painful,
even hostile and threatening. In my chrysalis dreaming, the
image of a rainbow comes to mind. In a playful way I imagine
all the colours of the rainbow fighting for supremacy, and I
realise what a ludicrous argument that would be. Suppose
one of them were actually to win the war and be king of the
palette. Imagine a world in just one colour – all brashly red, or
mellow yellow, all regal purple or shocking orange, all soothing

lavender or brooding indigo. I wouldn't want to inhabit such a world, not for more than a day, and the battle over which colour gets the prize would surely go on interminably. The rainbow resolves that conflict in an act of overarching beauty. This is the image that dominates my dreaming, inspired, I'm sure, by the sacred Spirit of Tomorrow. It tells me that there is a reality greater than all our arguments, in which our differences are not only overcome, but subsumed into what one might justifiably call Higher Definition.

What might define us more truly than all our differences? What is our rainbow in this disintegrating reality that is crumbling all around us? What is the Tomorrow that binds our differences and raises us to the skies? When our separate cells stop fighting each other and begin to join together into a greater unity, what will that look like? Could caterpillars really fly?

The Spirit of Tomorrow never gives me answers. She just opens up possibilities and invites me to consider them. She usually does it in pictures and stories. She knows how to penetrate the deeper reaches of my mind and heart – the place where lectures and sermons are generally denied admission. Today she tells me a story about a fence …

Once there were two neighbours who could never keep the peace between them. They quarrelled. They fought. They distrusted and eventually began to hate each other. One day one of them had had enough, and dug a deep ditch along the boundary of their adjoining strips of land, to stop the other ever approaching his territory. The second neighbour was so affronted that he called in a carpenter to erect a high fence along his boundary, so that he wouldn't see his neighbour's ditch every time he looked out of his window. Now this escalation of hostilities might have led to even worse divisions, had not the carpenter had ideas of his own. While his employer went to market, he took all the wood and nails he had been given and set to work. When the farmer came home, to his surprise and annoyance, he found not a fence but a bridge – carefully and artistically carved and spanning his neighbour's ditch.

Enraged, he railed against the carpenter, and was about to start pulling down the new installation, when he saw his neighbour coming towards him, already half way across the new bridge, and holding out a hand in friendship.

'Dear neighbour, I'm so sorry. In my spite against you I dug this ditch to keep you away, and now, far from retaliating in anger, you have had this beautiful bridge built to cross the gulf between us. Can we let this bridge be the start of a new chapter in our relationship?'

The carpenter had already moved on when the neighbours went to look for him – many more bridges to build. Perhaps he was the Spirit of Tomorrow. Perhaps he was a strange attractor – that unexpected, unscheduled possibility who makes the difference, resolves the conflict and can change the course of history. Such spirits come by many names and in all generations. Where will we find them in *our* generation, and in the midst of *our* conflicts?

Even in my chrysalis sleep I recognise the presence of that possibility. The conflict between the caterpillar system and the developing imaginal cells could never have been sustained. We would have used up all our energy for something ultimately destructive. But Nature knew better and raised us to a rainbow of our own.

And yet the conflict is real and needs to be addressed. Perhaps, once they had recovered from the shock of their unplanned meeting on the bridge, the two neighbours sat down together over a meal and a pint and thought over the reasons for their longstanding enmity. Perhaps they looked honestly at the root causes of their behaviour and quite possibly they discovered that two of the main suspects were fear and distrust of each other. Perhaps they looked at their very real and valid differences of opinion and considered what was more important to them – the issues that divided them or the values they held in common.

In the real world there is always a line to be negotiated. Working towards authentic unity never means diluting what really matters. It is more likely to involve a thoughtful blend of compromise and challenge. Where will I decide to co-operate with the views and the plans of the other and be willing to let go of some of my own rigid expectations and intentions? Where will I stand my ground and call out any issues and directions that are truly inconsistent with my own deeply-held values, hopes and dreams. Such negotiation is best conducted on neutral ground, in a congenial setting, and with the patience and mutual respect to talk – and to *listen* – for as long as it takes, which may well be no less than a lifetime.

What kind of rainbow bridge spans *your* dreams? Could its different colours ever find a way to rise beyond their difference to shape a greater wholeness? I seem to recall, from the times I've tuned into *SpiritFM*, that the human family in South Africa, where eleven languages are spoken, and racial tension and apartheid were once the norm, now call themselves The Rainbow Nation. What a triumph of the bridge over the fences.

THE BIGGER PICTURE

There's no shortage of time here in the chrysalis. Time to hang out and think. Time to reflect on the story of our life, on the times we struggled for our existence during the caterpillar time and on the terrifying disintegration that became this indescribable soup we are inhabiting here. It can all be more than a bit depressing. It's really hard to hold on to the hope of anything new coming to be. To be honest there are times when it feels completely impossible, and the darkness seems to move inside your mind. Maybe that's why the Spirit of Tomorrow visits our dreaming, to show us something that might open up for us beyond the mess we're in – to show us a bigger picture ....

My imaginal eyes are already drooping. I feel very weary these days. It might be the reaction to all the depressing signs around me, that seem to point to nothing good at all. But it could also be the weariness of advancing pregnancy, as that which is within me grows and grows, feeding on my energy to generate its own. What it will be is a mystery. I don't have access to any ultrasound scans. I just know that something new is evolving – a transformed creation is taking shape that will take the dreaming to another level, and maybe bring it to its fulfilment. Meanwhile I am simply weary, and sleep overcomes me once again.

Tonight's dreaming could have come straight out of 'Peter Pan'. The Spirit of Tomorrow takes me on a night flight to the stars. But this is no Victorian fairy story. It takes me to a place beyond even most human imagining. It takes me to outer space, and perches me, full of wonder, on the International

Space Station. The Spirit urges me, with her quiet irresistible persuasion, to listen to the response of some of the astronauts to their experience of space flight.

I watch as at first each of them points out his own country as they orbit the earth. After a couple of days they are pointing out not their countries but their home continents. Another few days and all they see is the earth itself. Lesser divisions are forgotten. If I could ask them where home is, they might begin by naming a nation but they would end by recognising that Earth is home, the one and only home they share. If you had asked me a short time ago where home is, I would have answered 'CaterpillarWorld'. But the Spirit of Tomorrow takes me on a flight far above CaterpillarWorld and now I must answer: Earth itself is my home. When all of us recognise Earth as home, then how could we continue to destroy any part of it for the sake of gaining power or resources for any other part?

Then I notice that many of the astronauts have tears in their eyes as they gaze at the Earth rising in the deep blackness of space – a delicate blue-green orb, infinitely beautiful, tenderly fragile, profoundly unique among the teeming galaxies. I hear them say that they will never be the same again, that this experience has changed them utterly. For the first time human eyes are seeing the human home from a great distance and, paradoxically, are feeling closer to it than ever before. From this distance the power struggles and territorial conflicts seem like playground scuffles, and yet …

… these observers know all too well that the continuing abuse, whether through wilful conflict or careless neglect, of this tiny globe hanging there in the darkness has the capacity to destroy it for ever, along with all the life it sustains. One of them tells the story of a band of thugs who set out to assault a beautiful girl. But when they came close and looked into her eyes they were overwhelmed by her vulnerable humanity, and instead of hurting her, they became determined to cherish and protect her. This, the Spirit shows me, is the kind of transformation, or conversion, that can happen when we are exposed to the bigger picture.

Ancient wisdom is full of stories about the bigger picture, and the challenging new perspective it brings to our hearts and minds. It speaks of those times when great kindness is shown to us precisely by those we had dismissed as beyond the pale – people who are 'not like us' and therefore suspect. It speaks of how the universe cherishes and sustains the tiniest wild flower as much as it cherishes and sustains the greatest intellect. It carries us to the mountain top, bids us look down at ourselves and our strivings, and see the wholeness of the web of life that binds us together. Such a flight can never leave you unchanged.

One astronaut comments that when you have once soared to the stars, your gaze will always be upward and outward, and you will never again be totally earthbound. His comments remind me of two people I once knew. One, who admittedly was always short of money, through no fault of her own, walked through life with her gaze constantly on the ground, where she not infrequently found coins that had been accidentally dropped. She found lots of coins that way, but how much she missed in the process – the migrating geese, the murmurations of starlings, the blue of the skies, the brooding grey of an impending storm, the lightning flashes, the wonder of the sunrise, the ever-changing cloud formations, the great sweep of the stars. It was a high price to pay for a handful of coins. The other was something of a romantic, people used to say. He went through life looking at the world above and around him. He saw new wonders every day. And all it cost him was a handful of coins.

'Look up,' says the Spirit of Tomorrow. 'No need to go into outer space. A hilltop will do nicely, or the view from your bedroom window or the reflection in the shining eyes of a child whose future stretches out ahead of her. Don't focus on the mud at your feet but on the skies above you. Look down, into negativity, and you may stumble. Look up, and tomorrow you shall fly.'

AFTERTHOUGHTS

K eeping dreams alive isn't for the faint-hearted. I'm supposed to be all about dreaming a future possibility – I'm an imaginal cell, but I tell you, I couldn't have kept the dream alive inside me without a lot of help from the Spirit of Tomorrow. The struggle to hold on to the deep truth I hold in my heart is probably nothing compared to your human struggle to hold on to your faith in the future when the chaos you are going through right now is taking fear and anger and desperation to a whole new level.

What helps me hang on in here through these deeply troubled times …?

- The kind of peace that comes from knowing that I'm not the saviour of the world, that it doesn't all depend on me, and sometimes what is asked of me is to keep quiet and let deeper energies prevail.

- The dawning realisation that this terrifying space between the No Longer and the Not Yet is a space of potential, not impotence, and that, ironically perhaps, as your Clarissa Pinkola Estes wisely remarks: *We were made for these times.*

- The assurance from ancient wisdom that authentic change happens one heart at a time, and that's what I can bring to the story – one heart, open to change.

- A recognition that all those One Hearts can join together in chains of human goodness and connectedness, linking small acts of kindness into global transformation.

- An honest acknowledgement of how I am really feeling, including the anger, the fear and the inevitable conflict. Only then can I begin to discern where I need to compromise and what I need to challenge and resist.

- Regular glimpses of the bigger picture, that come when I rise, for a moment, above the here and now with all its stresses, and gaze on what I see. I can't see the earth from outer space, but I *can* see the stars from the earth.

The Spirit of Tomorrow has one last challenge to whisper into my chrysalis dreaming, before, together, we embark on the enormous challenge ahead – the challenge to emerge from these times, bringing a new creation to the earth ....

You must become the future you long for.

PART 5
EMERGENCE

*'Loss makes artists of us all as
we weave new patterns in
the fabric of our lives'*

Greta W. Crosby

BIRTH STRUGGLE

'You must *become* the change you long for.' The words are still resonating in my heart as I start my great awakening. Realisation dawns on me with startling clarity and power: Truly I *am* becoming the change I long for!

For the first time in the course of this story, we get to overtake you, our human cousins, because this last leg of the journey takes us to the point of fulfilment – where we see what the journey has been all about. I know you haven't arrived there yet, which is why I'm inviting you to see what my caterpillar has become. My whole intention in doing this is to encourage you to keep going, to keep believing, and to assure you that there truly is something more than anything you can see at present or even imagine. If you can believe that caterpillars can fly, then believe also that humanity can evolve to a new level of consciousness. It's the same evolutionary dynamic of life itself that makes both these things possible.

So come with me now to the Labour Ward. We may be there for quite a while. If a human mother were on the Labour Ward for up to ten days, the medics might have to intervene, probably with a C-section. Not so for us. Our birth struggle goes on for between seven and ten days, as we wrestle to get free of the cocoon that has been enclosing us, and to emerge as a butterfly. In some ways these are the hardest days of all. To be apparently completely knotted up in the unyielding fibres that have held us suspended through the chrysalis time is even more frustrating than swimming aimlessly in the murky soup of the meltdown. You can see the light. You know now that you are becoming a butterfly, but you can't quite make the breakthrough.

However, human friends, please resist any temptation to

C-section us to speed up the process. There have been occasions when a well-intentioned observer has taken a pair of scissors and cut the strands that bound us. The thing is: we *need* the struggle. It's the struggle that gets the circulation going in our wings. If you cut short the struggle we will never fly. It seems perverse, perhaps, but think about your own life's journey, human cousins. When did you grow most? I mean *real* growth – inner growth, spiritual growth, not just feet and inches growth. If you look carefully you will probably find that the times of most intensive growth happened when you were dealing with the hard issues, in the stormy times not during the sunny intervals. When everything is going smoothly there is no incentive to grow and stretch your potential. Children only really learn something new in school when they hit problems. Pages of straight 'A' grades may please parents but they don't challenge the student to grow. We should be celebrating when we, or our children, make mistakes, because these are the learning points.

 ## EMERGENCE

A process by which larger, more complex entities arise out of the interactions of smaller or simpler entities; the process by which new order arises out of chaotic breakdown, so that new structures become apparent. Emergence occurs out of the disruption of existing systems, causing new possibilities to be revealed. This occurs typically in sudden quantum leaps in understanding or practice, constituting evolutionary shifts (such as the movement of life from ocean to land) or paradigm shifts in science, politics or theology.

The process of emergence is apparent, for example, in new technologies, new political narratives and, most importantly, in the evolution of human consciousness.

If the global crisis in which you now find yourselves is your human chrysalis, then the struggle to emerge from that crisis is itself an essential component of your evolution. A person who never struggles never truly comes to birth. Ancient wisdom tells us over and over again that there is always a price on the prize. The princess is only liberated by the one who has the strength, the courage and the persistence to struggle through the surrounding obstacles. The one who breaks through to a transformed existence is the one who has freely permitted life to break – sometimes violently – the fabric of the old existence. More recently your Viktor Frankl tells us: 'What doesn't break you makes you stronger.' You could turn that round and read the same truth: 'To become stronger you may need to let yourself be broken.'

Real strength, real power, comes from within – from the struggle to activate your wings, your true self. Beware the one who tries to impose power *over* you, using threats, playing on your fears, setting you one against the other, infecting you with hatred and distrust. That is not strength but the flaunting of an oversized ego.

Pay attention to the one who *enables* you, calls forth in you the strength and wisdom that is already inside you, empowers you from that source. Such people work through love, not hate. Ancient wisdom gives us a thumbnail sketch of how to recognise them:

They are more concerned for others than for themselves; they don't have an inflated ego; they don't force their view or ways on others; they are even-tempered; they seek the best in others, and don't take pleasure in others' faults and failings; they are tolerant and patient, rejoicing in everything that affirms life; they keep on going when the going gets tough and inspire others to do the same.

You might want to check out your human leaders against this blueprint for integrity. If you pick up the signs of a 'me-me, me-first' attitude you will know that such a one is always going to put his own advantage before the good of all creation. If you hear hate, bigotry and prejudice being preached; if you observe intemperate language and uncontrolled temper outbursts and constant attention-seeking, you are looking at either a toddler or a tyrant. Toddlers usually grow up. Tyrants only grow worse. If you come up against the force of will which indicates not inner strength but personal weakness, then take great care. A person's integrity quotient is usually in inverse proportion to the size of his or her ego.

Ancient wisdom tells us that divine strength is found in human weakness. If you seek leaders with integrity look for those who are gentle with others but firm with themselves, more eager to serve than to be pandered to, humble of heart but pursuing a genuinely exalted vision, always empowering, never over-bearing; able, as Kipling says, to look both success and failure, gain and loss, in the eye and not be seduced from the way of truth by either of those imposters.

Next time the ballot papers come round, think on these things.

You will see, as I take flight to the life for which I was born, that I am a great deal stronger than I appear. I gained that strength during my struggle to be born and to survive. I hope to use it in the service of all creation. But first I enjoy a short respite. I lie in the sunlight until my wings have dried out.

Why don't you rest a while now with me in the warmth, and gaze at the skies, and watch the future unfurl and I will tell you something of my new life with wings.

TAKING FLIGHT

As we bask here in the warm spring sunshine, I feel my whole being expanding, relaxing, and rising to something quite new. But I don't mind admitting that as the moment for change came closer, and I realised I was going to have to leave the shelter of the chrysalis time, I was scared. It was a different kind of fear from that caused, for example, by the risks to life from predators. Everything that lives on planet Earth has to deal with the fear that comes from simply trying to survive in what is often a dog-eat-dog world. This is true whether you are a caterpillar or a king.

No, this fear was something else. It was almost, one might say, *existential* fear. I knew that I had come to the brink of a whole new form of existence. I had reached the end of the road in my earlier form, and who was to say that there was anything else beyond that ... Or that if there *was* anything else, that it was something to be embraced with equanimity – it could be anything that lies beyond that curtain that we call death. Even though I knew, in my body and in my mind, that something new was growing inside me, I also knew that for that new being to emerge it would mean letting go of what I had always regarded as 'me'. I guess it was the ultimate identity crisis, and I'm sure this isn't something that is only felt in the caterpillar kingdom. To be on the brink of letting go of one form of existence without knowing what, if anything, lies beyond that brink, well, that has to be scary in anyone's book.

It's easy for me to share this with you here, on this grassy bank, as my new wings dry out in the sunshine. But I won't forget the fear I felt in the face of that 'passing over'. Your scientists, by the way, have discovered that butterflies have memories.

There are some sensory experiences that are retained from the caterpillar time to the butterfly time. Maybe it's important for me to share my fears with you, because each one of you, in the human realm, will also reach your own brink, when you will have to leave behind the earthly existence that has defined you so far. I can only speak for butterflies. I have no way of knowing what lies beyond the human brink. But my instincts tell me that nature is consistent in her patterns and processes. It would make no sense to me if human creatures were excluded from the miracle of metamorphosis, for which every humble caterpillar is created. Your wise thinkers call it spiritual evolution. My opinion, for what it's worth, is that you can trust it, without having to either understand it or know in advance where it is taking you.

But now, my friends, it's time to fly. My wings have become strong enough, through the birth struggle, and have dried out in the sun. I feel refreshed, and the fear has left me, because now I can see and experience for myself what it means to embrace this completely new, and yet mysteriously familiar, existence. I'm still who I am and who I always was. I have merely changed my form. Energy and matter/form, as your scientists have proved, are interchangeable. Moreover, they now know that energy cannot be created or destroyed. This means that what you see as 'death' is never extinction, but always just a change of form, a *transformation*. My old caterpillar form has returned to Energy and that energy, that eternal spirit of who I am has taken this new and amazingly beautiful winged form.

A gentle breeze caresses me. My brand new wings begin to flutter, and my whole body starts to rise on the currents of air. I weigh less than a gram. I feel extremely fragile, and yet somehow invincible.

The sensation of flight is wholly new to me. It quite literally takes me to heights I could never have imagined. It gives me such a sense of freedom – I can fly anywhere. And it gives me a whole new view of life, as I gaze down on the earth below. What I see almost takes my breath away. I rise up effortlessly through the forest at first, noticing the life that teems there. I'm the new kid on the block of course, but it doesn't take me long to spot the caterpillars. They take no notice of me. They have no reason to think I have any connection with their world. Why would they? For me it's a revelation. It's like looking down on my grandparents and my children all at the same time. It's a bit surreal.

The fact of the matter is that, of course, there is no way back, and there is no way that I can tell the caterpillars what lies ahead of them. From their perspective, I have simply disappeared, and there's no way I can explain the journey I have made so that they might understand, and see the future differently. I also pick up their troubles as I fly overhead. They are struggling with all the problems I faced myself in CaterpillarWorld, but from where I am now these problems look so different. Not that I would trivialise them – when you're a caterpillar these things matter so much – defending yourself against predators, getting more and more leaf, growing out of your skin and constantly expanding ... all of this is so very serious when you are embroiled in it, but now ...? I just wish I could reassure them that these caterpillar matters will pass, and they will one day see things so differently, and indeed become active participants in their own transformation.

I'm remembering the vision the Spirit of Tomorrow gave me, of the bigger picture. I look down and see no boundaries, no divisions, just the forest there for all, and the open skies spanning everything. All the conflict that goes on to safeguard these imaginary borders are caterpillar conflicts, and they are completely dissolved in the butterfly realm. It makes me wonder about your human problems and anxieties. How many of them are really caterpillar problems? Do you ever wonder whether these pressing questions that engage your energies will actually matter in a few years' time? And do you ask yourself whether your endless pursuit of caterpillar questions could be distracting you from the questions that really matter? How many of your personal and national decisions are actually based on caterpillar questions: 'How will this affect the interest rates or the price of cheap flights?' How often do your decisions engage with the bigger issues: 'What kind of society do I want to help establish? How does this course of action affect the planet and all the life it sustains?'

A wise soul once remarked to his anxious friend, 'You are fretting about so many things, Martha, but only one thing matters. Your sister Mary has chosen to focus on that one thing and let go the lesser worries.' I think he might have been thinking of caterpillar questions in a butterfly world. In CaterpillarWorld it's inevitable that there will be a lot of Martha-matters occupying our minds. But when we rise above them, we finally see things through Mary-eyes.

GIVING AND TAKING

The catering arrangements are very different here. In CaterpillarWorld, as you probably recall, it was a 24/7 'eat all you can' buffet. Here things are rather more refined. I've been issued with a piece of equipment called a proboscis. It's like a drinking straw on my head, and when I land on a flower it automatically uncoils and extends into the flower's nectary, where the treasure is stored. To think that I spent all my caterpillar days without any knowledge of the delights of nectar. I use my proboscis to draw out that food of the gods, and when I've finished, it coils back up again most conveniently.

It's a very different dining experience. The chomp and chew of CaterpillarWorld has given way to sip and savour – much more gentle and leisurely and discerning. I have discovered the joy of enjoying my food. I enter only those flowers that are open and welcoming of me and I do them no harm at all as I enjoy the nectar they freely offer me. I shudder to think how much damage I caused to the forest when I was a caterpillar.

And there's another thing. I'm generally considered to be very beautiful, though I say it myself, and I have hairy legs. I've noticed that something else happens when I land on a flower. The pollen inside the petals sticks to the hairs on my legs, and I carry it with me along to the next flowers I visit. I didn't plan this. It just happens, but the result is rather miraculous. I inadvertently pollinate the flowers that feed me. I think you call this a symbiotic relationship, in your human realm. For me it's a whole new way of looking at things – whereby both partners in a transaction are benefitted and enriched by it, and neither partner is diminished.

I'm reminded of something the Spirit of Tomorrow taught me in my dreamtime. Each single One can make a difference, and when many Ones work together the result is greater than the sum of the parts. All through the caterpillar time it was all about taking what we wanted. Now we still take what we desire, and what nourishes us, but we give something in return. We facilitate the next generation of the flowers by pollinating them. It affirms everything the Spirit of Tomorrow was trying to show me – that we move forward in our journey into the future by working together, and not by isolating ourselves, focusing on defence and protection all the time, living by the me-first approach. I'm also learning that a meal freely given and quietly enjoyed is so much more satisfying than the grab and snack methods of the past, where greed often spoke louder than need. Caterpillar life was frenzied, as we competed to get the next meal, destroying the table as we went. Now I'm able to live fully in the present moment, quietly participating in a mutually fruitful environment. I think you call it 'mindfulness'.

I guess I'm being a bit unfair on myself here. In fact of course we can't help the way we behave in CaterpillarWorld. It's the way things are. It's instinct and we don't know a different way. For you, my human cousins, that is not the case. Yet might there not be a lesson in spiritual evolution here for you? What might the Spirit of Tomorrow wish to say to you, if you have ears to hear? There are two simple questions you might ask, in any important decision: 'What is best for me, or for those I love?' *and* 'What is best for all creation?' For me this translates into: 'I can take the nectar that is good for me *and* I can contribute to the life of other parts of creation.' This is the kind of addition sum that wouldn't tax the ability of a six-year-old. It's an addition sum, not an either/or choice. And that's one of the characteristics of a higher level of consciousness – something only you, our human cousins, can achieve on this planet. Your wise ones call it non-dualistic thinking. It means growing beyond seeing life's situations through the either/or lens, and using the both/and lens instead.

Take the rainbow picture that I dreamed of in the chrysalis. Each of the individual colours thought it was all about them. They saw themselves through the lens of 'I (or my tribe or my country) am best and everything else is to be excluded or marginalised'. And then came the rainbow and said 'It's about *all* of you, no exclusions, no hierarchy.'

To live in a dualistic world is to see everything in black and white. As a caterpillar I lived in a world that paid no heed to the needs of other parts of creation. Once you have seen the world through butterfly eyes, everything reflects the whole spectrum of colour, of possibilities and potential, and nothing, not even those who disagree with you, can be excluded from the equation.

Until recently in HumanWorld, it seemed as though the message of give-and-take was beginning to take root, but there are worrying signs of regression. The message of a future of co-operation rather than conflict is being undermined by some of your leaders, and some of you are being seduced by their 'me-first' rhetoric into marching to a potentially sinister drumbeat. Countries and tribes are closing in on themselves, digging defences around themselves, pulling further away from each other, making it harder, not easier to work together, trade together, learn and grow together and co-operate in protecting and cherishing the planet. Some of you can see the warning signs. Not everyone wants it to be this way, and so you are bitterly divided against each other. The blade of division slices through friendships and families, communities and kingdoms.

It can't go on like this. You are teetering on the edge of your own cliff, and you desperately need some butterfly wisdom.

So don't just catch us in your nets and pin our lifeless wings to your specimen boards. Instead, follow our living flight, and let it inspire your own. Creation isn't yours to control and exploit, but it can be your wisest teacher. If you continue to take everything from the Earth without giving anything back, Nature will have to eliminate you from the equation, as she has done often in the past with destructive species. The rest of creation can survive very well without you, but you can't survive without us.

It doesn't have to end in tears. We can show you how to live in mutually life-giving relationship with each other. Watch and learn, before it's too late.

THE TRAVEL BUG

I 'm just a bug. I weigh less than a gram. I'm hardly a force to be reckoned with. But I love to travel. I *need* to travel. It's in my genes.

If I tell you that we delicate one-grammers, travel up to 9000 kilometres on our migration journeys, and that some of us can fly up to 100 kilometres in one day, you might shake your head in understandable disbelief. It does sound incredible but it's an example of so many of Nature's amazing journeys. The travel bug was already in evidence when I was a caterpillar. Sometimes we would crawl quite some way – by our standards – in our exploration of the forest, but wings, of course, take the travel to a whole new level.

As with our human cousins, we do short-haul, medium-haul and long-haul flights, depending on our type and size. As you will see from my image on the cover, I'm a Monarch, and we are definitely in the long-haul category – the 9000 kilometres return trip kind of flight. When I first emerged into my butterfly life I was a bit overwhelmed at the prospect of all the travel that lay ahead of me. The challenge raised all kinds of questions: 'Where are we going? How do we find our way? How will we get fuel for the flight?' And one last question that I didn't really like to voice: 'Will I really live long enough to make a journey of that duration?' The sad truth is that our life expectancy isn't very long. How many butterfly lifetimes would it take to fly from Mexico to Canada and back? (The answer is probably: 'about four', at which information you may well be raising your eyebrows.)

I can't even really start at the beginning, because this whole travel story is a continuing cycle, and you could slip into one of our flyways at several points along the way. Let me explain...

Down in Mexico it's hibernation time. We are pretty resilient, given our small size and fragile-looking bodies, but we don't do cold! If the temperature drops we move on, because frost would kill us. So we over-winter in Mexico where the temperatures remain manageable, and we sleep, clinging to trees, in huge swarms, for protection from the cold and from predators. When spring arrives in February or March we wake up, and our first waking thought is to find a mate. Then we embark on our long flight north and east and by March or April we are ready to lay our first batch of eggs so we look for the right kind of plant – we prefer milkweed – and lay them carefully, spreading them out between different plants to give them the best chance of survival.

Then comes the bad news. After laying our eggs, our own lives are over. The future of the journey is passed on to our children, who take up the flight when they have discovered their own wings, around May and June, and the baton passes to the next generation – and then, in July and August, to the next, and so on, until, from generation to generation, we have made the distance.

How do we do it, and why? Two very important questions. We have a built-in navigation system that would leave your human aerospace scientists jaw-dropped. We navigate as far as possible by the sun, but the sun isn't always in evidence, especially as we fly north, so we also use a very sophisticated magnetic GPS, picking up the earth's magnetic fields to estimate the time of day and our relative position. Of course, we know and understand nothing of all of this, and human research still hasn't fully worked it out. We simply follow our instinct and fly.

And why? Well there are two main reasons. We fly to find the best conditions for our survival, in terms of climate and available food. We follow the wild flower trail, through its changing seasons. But sometimes we also have to fly to escape from danger. For example, there are some very nasty parasitic wasps who like to insert themselves inside us, so that they grow within us and destroy us. Our cousins, the Painted Ladies, especially, have this problem.

So the answer to the 'Why?' is twofold: we are both economic migrants seeking better living conditions, and refugees fleeing mortal danger, just as it is in HumanWorld. And you know what? No one makes any distinction. We fly over infamous man-made walls at ten thousand feet and barely register them on our radar. We fly over and beyond all your man-made boundaries without a visa. No one checks our fingerprints or country of origin or forces us through unpleasant X-ray scanners. Wouldn't you like to travel like that?

And like all good journeys, ours takes us back, several generations later, to the very place – the very tree, from which our forebears set out, there to rest again before the next cycle begins.

As I contemplate the flight that lies ahead of me, I recall the message of the Spirit of my dreaming and the chains of kindness she showed me. Life, I discover, is very much like a relay race, whether you are a human or a bug. No one is asked to save the world single-handed (though some of your leaders seem to think they are), but the transformative power of love is passed on from heart to heart, life to life.

If a fragile creature weighing less than a gram can fly 9000 kilometres, then a flawed and fragile human race can become a carrier of peace, love and understanding, if the journey is shared along the generations and the wisdom to find the way is passed from parent to child.

Your late wise leader, Nelson Mandela, catches the truth of this perfectly:

'It always seems impossible until it's done.'

IMAGINING THE FUTURE

I've just laid the last of my eggs. I hope I've given them the best possible chance, placing them on the choicest milkweed. It's a bittersweet moment. It's such an amazing thing, to be able to give life to the future. But for me it's also laced with sorrow, because soon I will die. I have fulfilled my purpose and now I must hand the baton of life to the next generation.

In the short time that still remains to me, I find myself reflecting on the hopes and dreams I have for these children of mine. Perhaps you will be kind enough to indulge me, as I explore them, because I imagine that these reflections would be even more poignant for you, our human cousins, when you give birth. And of course you don't have to be physically a parent to be both fearful and hopeful for those who will come after you.

When you lay an egg, or birth a baby, you are committing a new life into a completely unknown future. It's a daunting prospect. Small wonder that so many new parents are terrified by the thought. In today's world that fear is very much amplified by global events and dangerous political directions that seem to be developing. It would be easy to see why fear might greatly outstrip hope. This kind of musing leads me to ask myself: What do I hope for for my descendants? What kind of future do I imagine, with my imaginal cell? What guidance would I want to give them to help them along the way ahead – a way that includes both nectar and wasps? It leads me also to invite you to ponder these questions for *your* descendants and the future inhabitants and custodians of our shared home.

148

IMAGINING THE FUTURE

I would want to warn my offspring that they will hatch into a world where there are many other creatures out to get them and that natural defences will be required. Every living creature soon learns that the rest of creation does not necessarily mean well. And I would have to mention that they will grow into greedy little grubs who will recklessly consume the very environment that supports them, that they will expand beyond all reasonable limits until they realise that they can't keep up this rapacious lifestyle. I will have to point out that this will lead to a terrible meltdown, in which they will think their entire universe is going to hell on a handcart.

So far it doesn't look much like a dream to be handing on. It looks more like a nightmare. So from the very beginning of their lives I would also tell them, if only I could, the great secret that they hold within themselves – the promise of a very different kind of world, curled up inside their imaginal cells. I would teach them to trust that promise, and by way of evidence I would show them my wings and tell them the story of my amazing journeys. I would assure them that if they dare but risk the flight they will be sustained along the way, dazzled by the sunlight, intoxicated by the sweetest nectar, cherished by humankind as bringers of hope. I would teach them that obtaining what you desire must go hand in hand with giving life to others. I would urge them never to harm a flower by force but always to wait for the right moment to be invited in.

I would tell them all of this, if I could, but before they hatch I will be gone. For you, my human friends, it is not so. You have the great privilege of time in which to get to know your children and grandchildren and to teach them the wisdom that life has placed in your own hearts. What are you dreaming for them?

They won't need you to show them how destructive human life is of this planetary home we share. They will see that for themselves. They won't need any instruction on the deadly effects of greed, reckless consumption, violent speech and action, ego-centric leadership or ruthless conflict. They will see it every day on television. They will be bombarded with it on social media. But by the same channels they will also pick up messages of protest, of hope and the possibility of change. Where they will need *you* is to provide wise guidance on how to navigate these perilous waters you call human life. Only from *you*, their elders, will they learn, as they grow up, how to choose between the destructive and the creative paths through life.

They may or may not listen to what you say, but they will be far more profoundly influenced by who you are. If you are to convince them that there is a better, more life-giving way, you will need to show them your wings! Don't you believe you have wings? Then let me ask you: How did humanity fly this far? How did you move beyond the horrors of the medieval period? How did you discover the importance of education and universal health care? How did you (albeit very slowly) learn the importance of tolerance and the art of listening to those who may not share your opinions, of debating important issues, leading to the beginnings of democratic government? How did you learn to respect minorities in your midst, and protect their rights and to cherish the welfare of the planet itself? Who taught you to reject all violence as a solution to your problems and to strive for peaceful and civilised solutions instead? Who urged you to open your borders to those fleeing persecution, and even to question your right to erect those borders in the first place, given that you first took the land you now call yours from other peoples who had settled there long before you arrived?

You did all this, my friends, by *becoming the change you longed for*. You will pass on this transformative potential to those who come after you by demonstrating its power in your own lives, your own generation, your own place and time. Of course the process of your spiritual evolution is still woefully incomplete, but the call is there, moment by moment, tightly enclosed in your own imaginal cells. They not only know the future fullness, but they already contain it. Don't ridicule them or call them trouble-makers. Listen to the prophetic voices within you and around you. Shun the evil wasps who get under your skin and lay the seeds of discord, conflict and hatred in your hearts. I think you know who they are, and what they look like and sound like in HumanWorld. I think you recognise the tone and menace of their rhetoric.

The future you dream of for those who come after you may seem as remote and unimaginable to you today as the butterfly seems remote and unimaginable to the caterpillar. Look at me and you will see that it is actually closer to you than your own next breath, waiting only for its moment to unfurl its wings in a world that lives by very different values from those that prevail at present on the planet we all call home.

The great secret, known deep in the heart of the imaginal cell, is that new life emerges out of great turbulence and that the only way to discover it is to plunge into the turbulence and trust it to bring forth its fruit. This secret is hidden in plain sight; in human experience, in physics and mathematics, in the natural world and in ancient wisdom. There, for example, we find a strange story about a pool of water in the old city of Jerusalem. Those who were sick believed that every so often the waters of the pool would become agitated by the touch of an angel. A person who entered the waters during these stormy periods would be healed and restored. Perhaps this is also a story for our times. The storm angel is here in force, but there is a great gift hidden in troubled times, and, like a treasure on the ocean floor, it will only be found by those who have the courage and the trust to enter the waters.

So this would be my last word to my still unhatched children: 'Don't be afraid of the turbulence, for it holds new life. You can't stay in the egg. You can't remain in your caterpillar form. You can't be a chrysalis for ever. Trust your imaginal cells. Plunge into the waters of transformation because you are born to fly.'

POSTLUDE
TAKING IT FURTHER ...

*'It may be that when we no longer
know which way to go
we have come to the real journey ...
The impeded stream is the one
that sings'*

Wendell Berry

Our guide has died, but not before laying a new generation of eggs. A chapter has ended and a new one begun. In the butterfly world evolution may well have reached its climax, but this is certainly not the case for *homo sapiens*. We are still very much a work-in-progress, and at times, especially in our own times right now, it can feel more like a work-in-regress.

The butterflies lay their eggs carefully in the optimum environment for their future development. Has our species any less of an advantage? Have we not likewise started the journey of life on a Goldilocks planet, where conditions are 'just right' for evolution to proceed, providing a perfectly balanced environment for our development and plenty of difficulties to challenge us and stimulate our creativity as we strive to overcome them?

Yet there is still a very large gap between *homo sapiens* and 'the human being, fully human and fully alive'. A story is told of a group of explorers and the indigenous companions who supported them and carried their equipment. The first few days went very well, and the explorers made rapid progress towards their destination. But one morning the native companions failed to report for duty. On investigation, it was discovered that they were taking a rest day. When the explorers protested, pointing out the urgency of the project, the simple reply was this: 'We have made record speed so far, at your insistence. But now it's time to pause, and let our souls catch up with us.'

The challenge of spiritual evolution is exactly that: to let our souls catch up with us. While we frantically accelerate our race through life, fruitlessly trying to stay ahead of the juggernaut of advancing technology and a suffocating avalanche of information, we have lost a child. We have become disconnected from the divine child called Wisdom, the source of our spiritual growth and the essence of our humanity. She is sheltering deep in our souls crying out to us to pause and search for her, and walk hand in hand with her again as nature intended. We too need to pause and let our souls, with their precious cargo, catch up with us.

This is the chrysalis challenge – to hang on in there, to wait, but also to invest more energy than ever in the task of growing and giving birth to our own wings and becoming who we were born to be. It won't happen just by passively waiting for the universe to shift us back into gear, although this will be an important component. It also requires our active, intentional and intelligent co-operation. We too face a birth struggle.

We are co-creators of humanity's future, so what do we want that future to look like? What kind of world do we truly desire? What dreams does the Spirit of Tomorrow suggest to our hearts? And how can we live in such a way that those dreams move a little closer to fulfilment? The question that now confronts us is how to play our own part, both individually and collectively, in this great work.

If any of the issues and possibilities raised in this book have fired your imagination, and you are wondering how to turn the promise of transformation into a practical reality, you might like to take the journey further with the follow-up companion book:

Born to Fly: A Handbook for Butterflies-in-Waiting

Finally, may the Irish, who perhaps understand more than most on this planet how to let their souls catch up with them, bless our striving with Celtic wisdom:

POSTLUDE

May the sun enlighten us with daily renewed hope
May the rain of peace and justice fall softly upon our hearts
May the winds of change be ever at our back,
May the road towards a better future rise to meet us,
May the universe mean well with us,
And may the Sacred Spirit grow us into the best we can be
Holding us gently in the palm of her hand.

Published in November 2017

BORN TO FLY
A HANDBOOK FOR BUTTERFLIES-IN-WAITING

www.dltbooks.com